rock bottom is a
beautiful
place

testimonies of triumph

by Diane Cunningham

For more information, please email info@nacwe.org.

Published by:
Diane Cunningham
2140 E Southlake Blvd, Suite L-643
Southlake, TX 76092

ISBN-10: 1-940847-73-7
ISBN-13: 978-1-940847-73-3

ROCK BOTTOM IS A BEAUTIFUL PLACE

Acknowledgments

"It is not about you." That is what God had to remind me during the process of this book. It is about the story. It is about the transformation. It is about the miracles. It is about each of us.

Thank you, God, for sobriety and the gift of recovery. Thank you, God, for all of the ways that I have seen You work miracles in my life since my Rock Bottom week. Thank you, God, for each "one day at a time" that I have been given. I am yours and I will keep walking, talking, and teaching this message as You lead me.

To my amazing editor for this project, Hanne Moon, who sent me virtual coffee, chocolate, and hugs on the days that I felt like I could not keep going. Hanne's story is also in the book, so be sure to read about her journey.

To the Rock Bottom women, you are talented, brilliant, resilient, and beautiful. I love each of you. Your stories matter. This book is changing lives. I can't wait to read your book where you share more about what you have learned.

To my family, who have loved me in the good and the bad for over forty years. Thank you for loving me during my rock bottom week as I gathered myself up and tried to pick up my pieces.

To my friends, the ones who knew me before and the new ones that have come from my Rock Bottom experience. Thank you for walking this path with me. Thank you for sitting in the rooms with me, sharing your story with me, texting me, talking to me when I have "fallen off the beam." I love you!

To all who walk the Rock Bottom path, which is all of us, may we see the beauty in each other and shower each other with grace.

To those still hurting, wandering, and wondering…welcome home. You are loved!

ROCK BOTTOM IS A BEAUTIFUL PLACE

Contents

Introduction

Rock Bottom Is A Beautiful Place was born on a summer day as I was journaling about my day in a Starbucks in Southlake, Texas before going to my meeting. As I walked through (and continue to walk through), my own "one day at a time," I began feeling the need to share my message. I began to want to share it in public with my tribe of people. I didn't know if this was a good idea or more of my insane behavior. But I continued to feel this prompting from God to STOP being silent.

It was the SILENCE that led me to drink.

It was the SECRETS that led me to feel like I was being a fake.

It was the years of TRYING TO HOLD THINGS TOGETHER and look good to the world, being THAT girl I was supposed to be, that led me to my rock bottom week.

I finally decided to begin sharing. I have shared bit by bit, piece by piece. The people in my inner circle found out right away. Then I began telling people in circle after circle. I told some of my private clients. I told my women leaders from the National Association of Christian Women Entrepreneurs (NACWE). I told my members. And with each telling came more freedom. I am a woman of God. I am a leader of women. I am a person of influence. If this influence can help another woman not get stuck in shame or silence or victimhood, then my sharing is the right thing.

When I got really brave, I shared my story in public at the NACWE *Catch on Fire* conference and offered women the chance to join me in writing this book by sharing their stories too. The response was nothing short of a miracle for me.

Women were ready. Women came forward. Women, just like me, broken and wounded, but full of grace and power.

Then on March 1st, I posted on my Facebook profile that I was sober. Using that word on social media was a milestone for me. One step at a time. One day at a time. Each act of bravery building upon the one before.

At this moment, the video that I lovingly call "my alcohol video" is live on YouTube. Was that a scary moment for me? YES, I must tell you that it was. But each time I watch myself telling my own story on this video, I see GRACE. I see a woman whom I've come to know and love. I see God using me. I see hope and healing.

I have been warned against sharing this information with you about my addiction. Why? Well, I've been warned against this because I might "fall off the wagon" and drink again. I totally get that. I am living one day at a time, working the steps, following the program that has worked for millions of others. I willingly admit that I could go drink today. Or next week or a year from now. But I'm not willing to wait to share this message. In fact, I feel compelled to share this with the world.

Rock bottom is rock bottom. It is tragic and ugly, and I felt utterly horrified at myself on that day. But that day and that disgust finally got me willing to consider that I might have a problem. And then willing enough to be humble and ask for help. As it so eloquently states in the "big book" of Alcoholics Anonymous, "All of us felt at times that we were gaining control, but such intervals—usually brief—were inevitably followed by still less control, which led in time to pitiful and incomprehensible demoralization."

These words made perfect sense to me.

- My background as a counselor didn't keep me from rock bottom.
- My master's degree and certifications and accolades didn't keep me from rock bottom.
- My moving to a new place didn't keep me from rock bottom.
- My multitude of friends, followers, and fans didn't keep me from rock bottom.

Are you a Christian businesswoman who would like to have the fellowship and support of fellow Christian women entrepreneurs? Visit us at www.nacwe.org to join the fastest growing network of women just like you.

- My hundreds of hours of going to counselors, support groups, retreats, and trainings did not keep me from rock bottom.

Not even my family could keep me from rock bottom.

As they say in the recovery rooms, the only meeting you are ever late to is your first one. We get where we need to be, in God's perfect timing. I got to my day of freedom on June 19, 2013. I found out recently that June 19th is Juneteenth, a holiday in the United States that is also called Freedom Day or Emancipation Day. It commemorates the announcement of the abolition of slavery in 1865. I find this to be so interesting. God set me free that day too. And I'm so very grateful for my rock bottom.

What is Rock Bottom?

Rock Bottom looks different for each of us. You will see that as you read through these stories. This book is a movement. It is women sharing things they have never shared before. It is full of pain and purpose, tragedy and turning points. As I've read through each story submitted, I've sat and cried. The words I've written down in the notebook next to me are in no particular order—just what I saw and felt as I went through the manuscripts…

Raw—authentic
Learning to ask for help
Medical diagnosis
Children
Weight
Peeling off the layers
Brokenness
Melding of business and life
Ache
Hunger
Jealously
Restless, irritable, and discontent
It wasn't about me
Broken hearts

Limiting beliefs
Addictions
Bondage
Chains
Divine appointments
Surrender
Death of a child
Questioning God
Severe mercy
Living testimony
Create masterpieces
Refiners fire
Learned to dance in the fire
Willingness

I am in awe of how this book has come to life. I pray for courage for each woman as we keep walking side by side. I wholeheartedly know that God's grace sets us free.

This book is a testimony…my testimony and the testimony of many.

The miracles are in each day, in each story, in each woman.

We want to hear from you after you read it. That is the gift you can give back to us.

If you are tempted to judge us, you are in the wrong place.

We don't need judgment and neither do you. We've walked through that and have already endured plenty of it from our own negative self-talk and the judgments of others. If you are here to support another broken soul that is loved by God, stay around.

To those of you that are still hiding, running, and hoping no one will see how broken you are…

I understand. It was me too. I know that sharing this message is controversial. I know that you might want to judge me. I challenge you NOT to. I encourage you to think before you do that. I am just like you. I am just willing to share my message in a BIG public way. I feel that this is what God has asked me to do.

Share with Us

Every woman has a story. We know you have a story too. We invite you to come and join us as you rise up victorious. Share your message. Speak your truth. Stop hiding.

Be a part of our next book in the Rock Bottom series. We plan to continue sharing a message of our experiences, strengths, and hopes. We would love for you to come with us….

Find out more here: www.rockbottomisabeautifulplace.com

Rock Bottom...

...My Story

It's not enough to invite Jesus into your mind. You have to open the door to your heart of hearts. No door can remain unlocked. Even the door to your secret room.
– Mark Batterson

Diane Cunningham

My rock bottom day was June 19, 2013. I was disgusted, ashamed, and humiliated—as well as enduring the extreme pain of the worst hangover of my life. You see, the night before I drank an entire liter of tequila by myself. But it wasn't just that one night. Alcohol and I had been good friends for many years.

My addictive personality first found solace in food. Food took care of me. Food comforted me. I could hide in food. And this is where I first waged my addiction war.

It started with food and my body in my growing up years. Weight gain, weight loss, anorexia, Overeaters Anonymous, and a month of inpatient treatment, all by the age of eighteen.

My addictions have been many—food, shopping, relationships, work, people. I have been addicted to other peoples' opinion of me, my image, who I think you want me to be. I have been addicted to positive (or better) things, including running, reading, and coffee.

You get the idea.

The alcohol was what brought me to my knees and all the way to rock bottom. And as the founder and president of the National Association of Christian Women Entrepreneurs, I certainly didn't want you to know about my "problem." In fact, most of the time, I really didn't think I had a problem. You see, I was able to "control myself" or "cut back." There were times that I would go on a binge-drinking episode, and then I would stop for a few days. One time I went a month without drinking, and another time I went seventeen days. But then I'd go back to my regular routine of daily drinking each night. As I look back, I realize I had been drinking daily for about fifteen years. It was only after some embarrassing episode that I would put myself "on restriction."

The ironic part is that I had been in and out of 12-step programs for twenty-two years (Overeaters Anonymous, Debtors Anonymous), worked in a hospital in the chemical dependency unit, led support groups as a counselor, and had been in a relationship with someone with an addiction. I just felt that I knew better, or understood, or could handle it. Plus, I didn't suffer many consequences that anyone could see.

After my divorce in 2011, the drinking increased. I had no one to see my nightly routine and my drinking. The pain of the loss of my ten-year marriage, the fact that I had no children, and then the death of my 13-year-old dog Bear all contributed to me turning to alcohol for comfort. Add on top of that trying to support myself financially, dating on occasion, and just trying to be the woman I thought I needed to be for everyone—well, it was a recipe for disaster.

The drinking started each night at 5, 6 or 7, depending on what I had going on. Towards the end of my drinking career, most of it was me alone in my rental home, listening to music, talking on the phone, texting, painting, or watching an occasional television program.

My rock bottom week was on a vacation to California to visit my family (my parents, my sisters, their husbands, and their kids). Looking back, I know I was feeling sorry for myself and left out. I was the only one divorced with no kids, and the emptiness just seeped into me, but I had no way of saying that. I loved being Auntie Texas to my nieces and nephews, but as I drank margarita after margarita by the pool at our timeshare from two in the afternoon until ten that night, I was not acting like a good aunt. I woke up at two o'clock in the morning by the pool, my iPhone stolen, locked out of the timeshare, and having to wake up my entire family to get back in. That was my last drink. I made it two weeks using the "white knuckle method" until I got to my first AA meeting. I am eternally grateful that I was willing to walk through those doors.

I started writing about this experience two days afterwards on the plane home from my trip. Here is what I wrote:

Friday June 21st

I know what "rock bottom" looks like now. Today is day three of my re-entry from that day. This is my story. I am going to spill my guts. As a good Christian girl, and the founder and president of a Christian company, this is not the story I want to be writing. It has been a slow slide into this place. Glimpses have risen to the surface over the past two years. I have teetered. I have made agreements with myself. I have asked for forgiveness the next morning. I have had to retrace my steps, find my keys, re-read my texts.

My name is Diane and I don't want to admit this, but I do believe that I am an alcoholic. Writing it makes it real. I have not said it this week. I have danced around the "A" word when talking about what happened. People have had to rescue me this week. My family has made excuses for me. My sister told my nieces, whom I cherish, that the reason I was locked out of the room without a key was because I was sleepwalking.

This is my truth. I am typing this as I sit on an airplane back home to Texas. Now it gets worse, but I wanted you to ease into this with me. I am afraid you aren't going to like me anymore. I am also afraid to say goodbye to my friend "A". I know that "A" is waiting at home for me and I am going to need to say goodbye. I know that I still have messes to clean up from "my rock bottom night" on Tuesday. Today is Friday.

I had two events this week that showcased my problem for all to see. The first was on Sunday night and the second was on Tuesday night. I did binge drinking both nights. I did this all on my own accord, with no one to blame for making me the drinks. It was all me. I know I have an addictive personality. It became even more obvious to me during these events.

I am afraid right now. "A" has gotten me through, has been my support, my friend, my comfort. "A" is my abusive relationship, my love affair. "A" is my dark side, my secret wild side that can't come out. Who am I without it? I don't know. I know that I just need to take it one day at a time, like the program teaches. I know I need to go to the program. I am scared to death.

What I am afraid of losing?

Who am I?

Will I still be fun?

I need to remember the horrible feeling of shame. I don't ever want to forget that shame and guilt-filled morning.

Here is what I remember: Waking up by the pool on a lounge chair. A young man sitting near me, three chairs down. I walk inside the timeshare and go to the ladies' room on the first floor. I then realize I don't have my phone. I walk back outside to where I was and there is no phone. The man, in his mid-20s, is still there. I talk to him, asking him if he saw a phone. He says no. I am still very drunk, but begin walking around. I go to the room to look for my phone and realize that I don't have a key. I walk down to the lobby and talk to Michael (who is working the front desk) and tell him that I can't find my cell phone. I tell him that I woke up and I was sitting near the young man outside. I am sure I look and sound like a crazy person, or rather a drunk woman.

I walk around outside again. The young man is gone. I look all around the pool, everywhere. I walk back inside and look in the bathroom. No phone. I finally go to ask Michael to call room 207 and have them let me into the room. My sister and dad both wake up and let me into the three-bedroom unit we are all sharing. I get a key. They go back to sleep. I leave and go look again for my phone. I search everywhere. It is 2 a.m. I *am drunk. I can't think. I am praying silently and asking God to help me, and the tears start. Then I realize that I was talking on the phone and texting. Who was I talking to? What was the last conversation? What were the last texts?*

I get back to the room and I go to sleep. Feeling naked without my phone. My seven-year-old niece, Emily, wakes me up at about 6 a.m. I tell her that I can't find my phone. I walk outside with her and look. Michael is still at the front desk. I ask him about my phone again. I look all around again. I ask the man cleaning the pool. I look in the garbage cans.

You see, this phone is how I run my life, my business. It has 4000 photos on it. I have a call for my company at 10 a.m., in just a few hours. I don't know if the phone is lost or if the guy that was sitting near me stole it. I have no clue. I do know that I have a giant headache. I talk to my sister and my dad and tell them what has happened. I use my sister's phone to call AT&T and cancel my phone. In the midst of this, I realize that I drank the entire bottle of tequila all by myself. Yes, twenty ounces. My head hurts as I type this, and it is three days later.

As the morning wears on, I'm in a haze, trying to make decisions, trying to act normal in front of my family, and lead a conference call. I walk to the coffee shop with my dad and sister. I get a bagel. I drink coffee. I have no phone. I am disgusted. Humiliated. I am broken. I am weak. I tell my sisters and my dad to not tell my mom. That I will tell her myself later. You see, I embarrassed myself on Sunday night too.

On Sunday night, I was inebriated from drinking twelve straw-ritas. Yes, a twelve-pack all myself. I started early that day. I think I had my first ones at about one or two o'clock. By 6 p.m., I was tanked up. I was talking by phone. I was texting. I was down by the pool, sitting on the balcony. But in the midst of that, my family decided to hold a "family meeting." My parents (who are divorced), me, my two younger sisters, and their husbands. I only remember parts of it. I had to ask them the next morning what had happened. It was that day my mom told me she was worried about my drinking. Monday.

So to recap, on Sunday, I drank twelve straw-ritas. On Monday, I had no alcohol to redeem myself with my family. On Tuesday, I managed to outdo myself again with the tequila.

Here is what I know for sure…

- *I have bruises on my shins right now that I can be assured I got on Tuesday night. I don't remember when or where.*
- *I lost my phone and went to buy a new one and my Dad got it for me. I don't know what is more embarrassing. The entire episode or the shame of my father having to pay $450 for a new phone for me.*
- *I am lucky that I was not raped.*
- *I am lucky that I did not fall into the pool, or walk into the street, or leave the premises.*
- *I am lucky that I did not die from too much alcohol.*

Just reading what I wrote makes my stomach hurt today…I was "soul sick."

I have learned so much since that day. Since then, my life has changed. I am sober and living one day at a time. I have been writing about my experiences in a journal. I am working the twelve steps suggested as a part of Alcoholics Anonymous, meeting with my sponsor, attending meetings, and making amends. I am living with a newfound freedom. I have nothing else to hide.

I began to share my story with my clients, my friends, and my colleagues, little by little, person by person. A few short months after I got sober, I realized that I needed to share my message with the world. As a person with influence, I feel a calling on my life to be authentic. I recorded a video testimonial about my rock bottom in September and released that on YouTube and to the public in February. This book is the next part of the puzzle.

God has rescued me from alcohol, depression, divorce, the pain of infertility, food, and so much more.

I have found my true rock is not about rock bottom, it is about finding out that God is my Rock and He was waiting for me all along. He is my safe place, not found in a bottle of wine, vodka, or anywhere else.

The LORD is my rock and my fortress and my deliverer,
My God, my rock, in whom I take refuge;
My shield and the horn of my salvation, my stronghold.
I call upon the LORD, who is worthy to be praised,
And I am saved from my enemies.
The cords of death encompassed me,
And the torrents of ungodliness terrified me.
The cords of Sheol surrounded me;
The snares of death confronted me.
In my distress I called upon the LORD,
And cried to my God for help;
He heard my voice out of His temple,
And my cry for help before Him came into His ears.
Psalm 18:2-6 (NASB)

By telling you this, my fear is that you will know who I can be and what I am capable of. My first concern was that I was going to lose my business and the company that I have worked so hard to create with women whom I love.

I know that rock bottom is a beautiful place because God has set me free to share this with the world. My story is not for me, it is for you. It is for us. It is a story of forgiveness, surrender, and learning to be totally me.

For by grace you have been saved through faith. And this is not your
own doing; it is the gift of God (Ephesians 2:8 ESV).

I love Rock Bottom. God is my Rock. I pray that you will find healing, authentic vulnerability, and the willingness to surrender whatever might be holding you back.

We are praying for you. You are loved.

Rock Bottom is indeed a Beautiful Place.

He has sent me to bind up the brokenhearted…proclaim freedom for the
captives…release from darkness for the prisoners…comfort all who mourn…
to bestow on them a crown of beauty instead of ashes, the oil of joy instead of
mourning, and a garment of praise instead of a spirit of despair…for the
display of His splendor (Isaiah 61 NIV).

ROCK BOTTOM IS A BEAUTIFUL PLACE

Enough

You may encounter many defeats, but you must not be defeated. In fact, it may be necessary to encounter the defeats, so you can know who you are, what you can rise from, how you can still come out of it. – Maya Angelou

Sylvia Alonzo

Have you ever had something in your life that you were afraid or ashamed to tell anyone about, a secret that you had tucked inside and imbedded in the deepest part of you so that it had no chance of getting out? I carried mine for seventeen years, but it would be someone else's secret that would change our lives forever.

We were a family of seven, so bedtime at our house was like a scene from *The Waltons* television show, with everyone saying goodnight to everyone. One November evening, after all the goodnights were said, my oldest daughter Isabelle came into my room complaining of an aching stomach. Certain that it was the result of the late night snack consisting of chips and dip, I sent her off to bed. The following morning Isabelle was feeling worse, so after leaving the other kids off at school, my husband dropped us off at the hospital emergency room. The pain was getting worse, and now I was getting worried.

Isabelle was a quiet girl and a straight "A" student. She was also quite the athlete. She tried out for almost every sport in school and made the team each time. She pushed herself and excelled. That day at the emergency room, she was more quiet than usual. I thought it was because she was in so much pain.

"Mom, why does it hurt so much?" she asked.

"Let's wait for the doctor and see what he says," I said. The doctor came in he asked the usual questions, asking what hurt and for her to describe her pain. Then he asked, "Could you be pregnant?"

She glanced at me in silence. The doctor walked out of the room and I asked her if she was pregnant. She didn't speak. She only shook her head. "If you are pregnant, just let me know. Don't worry about dad. I'll take care of him," I told her.

I had met my husband at church. We started dating when we were sixteen years old and were married when we were twenty. He was handsome, soft-spoken, and seemingly mild mannered. Isabelle was born within the first year of our marriage. It was also within the first year that the violence began.

That was my secret, the one I had tucked away so deeply so that no one would ever know. I can't tell you how many times I was pushed, humiliated, hit, or punched, but I do remember the first time. Isabelle was one month old. We lived in a studio apartment and had very little money. It was a Friday, payday, and I waited for my husband to get home from work, but he didn't come home. He finally came home on Sunday, but without a paycheck.

We had a newborn that needed diapers and formula, and we argued. He lost it, shoving me so hard that I fell back and hit my head on the wall. I was stunned. That day and that feeling were singed in me. No one could know what had just happened. Every memory of every incident (the time he broke my hand, the night he woke me up by squeezing my neck, the time he put out his cigarette on my wrist), I tucked away, right along with the first memory, so that no one would know that I was not worth caring for, not worth loving. I felt such shame. I couldn't tell anyone. I was afraid of what they would think of me if they knew. They might think I was to blame or that I was not worthy enough to love, and then they would also stop loving me. After all, I had been told that time and time again.

Not every day was bad. There were good times. But knowing what kind of mood he would be in or what would set him off on any given day was a guessing game. We were anxious all the time.

"Are you pregnant?" I asked again.

"I can't tell you. It's bad," she said.

"If it's a baby, we'll deal with it. If you want to finish school, I'll help you take care of it. If the boy doesn't want to help you, I'll adopt the baby. It's going to be okay."

"No," she said, "its dad."

"What about dad?" I asked.

"He makes me do things," she said.

I stood in silence for a moment. I was stunned. A child should never utter those words, and they had just come out of my daughter's mouth. Her secret was out. There was no time to process the news I was just given before the doctor came out of the exam room to tell me that my daughter was in labor. I fell to the floor in the corridor and sobbed. A nurse walked over to me and asked if she could give me a hug.

"I don't deserve one," I answered. I felt like a failure. I had failed my daughter. I was broken.

There are things about that day that I don't remember clearly. But I do remember vividly my husband walking up the hallway when he got to the hospital to check on my daughter. He saw the officers standing guard at my daughter's door and fled. He knew the secrets were out.

My daughter gave birth to a beautiful baby girl. She had decided to give the baby up for adoption and didn't want to see or hold her. I spent the next couple of days at the hospital with my daughter, and every now and then I would sneak into the nursery to hold the baby and whisper to her that I loved her. My heart broke at the thought of giving her up. When the day came for my daughter to give the baby to the caseworker, my daughter asked me to adopt her baby. None of what was happening made any sense.

Our lives after that can only be described as organized chaos. I was now going to be raising six kids by myself. There were investigators, child protective services, doctors, counselors, and court proceedings. My husband was given an eighty-eight year prison sentence. We could all finally breathe.

The next few years were difficult, but seemed to go well. We moved from New Mexico to Texas, and at the insistence of my sister, we started going to church. I thought I had tucked away the hurt, fear, guilt, and shame but every now and then, they reared their ugly heads. Anger and bitterness were my only friends. I put up walls. If no one could get in, I couldn't be hurt again. I was severely depressed. No one knew I had become addicted to the medication I had been prescribed for anxiety and depression. I was taking large quantities of pills so that I could numb the pain and quiet the memories.

One night, as I was getting ready for bed, I heard all the kids laughing down the hall. It was at that moment that I knew I had to move on. They had. My daughter graduated high school in the top 10 percent of her class and got a full academic scholarship for college. The other five kids were thriving. I knew I had to make some major changes for them and for me.

Change didn't happen instantly. I asked God to help me make sense of the mess, and slowly and steadily God started shifting things in our lives. I started by getting off the prescription medication. After getting fired from my job, being unemployed and on public assistance for over a year, I went into business for myself. Soon I began to pray for God to help me deal with those things I had tucked away for so long—the anger, fear, pain, and the inability to forgive. They have not magically disappeared, but every day that I lay them at God's feet, they become less and less.

I have learned to trade the things that I believed about myself for the truths of God's word. I prayed for friends and mentors whom I could share my story with, and God connected me to people who were encouraging and loving. I prayed for God to heal my children completely. My two older kids, Isabelle and Eddie, are married and have children of their own. Martha and Daniel recently graduated high school. Annie is a fierce high school softball player and Arielle (which means "Lion of God") is a quirky ten-year-old honor roll student. The journey isn't over; we were still in counseling even as of last year. But it's a different journey now.

The road to recovery is hard. It's hard to verbalize your pain because not everyone will understand. I lost a few friendships because they couldn't or wouldn't deal with the mess that was my life. But there is hope. God's grace is enough. There is freedom in Christ. He makes all things new. Trade the lies, the shame, and fear for God's truths. You are loved. You are forgiven. You have a purpose. Speak up and ask for help if you find yourself in an abusive situation. You are a child of the Almighty God. You are enough.

Sylvia Alonzo is the owner of MDXchange, L.L.C. She is the sole parent of six really fun people and grandmother to Sophia, Nathan, and Isaac. Sylvia has a special place in her heart for single moms who are or have been in abusive relationships, and has a driving desire to let them know that there is freedom in Christ. www.mymdxchange.com

ROCK BOTTOM IS A BEAUTIFUL PLACE

How My Lowest Led Me to His Highest

Rock bottom became the solid foundation on which I rebuilt my life. – J. K. Rowling

Silvia Perez Arvelo

I hated what he was wearing: white socks, black shoes, and light blue pants. It was November 30, 1986. I was the pastor's daughter sitting in Sunday school when this new guy walked in. If you've been in a church setting long enough, you know that the new guy gets the attention of *all* the girls. He ended up winning my heart, my family's heart, and our church's heart. On January 23, 1987, I became his girlfriend, and yes, he stopped wearing both the pants and the socks.

Eighteen months later, we were madly in love and saying "I do" to each other at the church where my parents were pastoring. We were married by the same minister who married my parents. It was special and perfect, just the way we both imagined our wedding day. About three months after our wedding, we found out I was pregnant with our first child. We were thrilled!

Before our first wedding anniversary, we were holding a beautiful baby girl. I thought, *Can life get any better than this?* This is what most of us women dreamed of when we were little girls, right?

We were able to enjoy those precious moments just a little while longer.

One Saturday afternoon, my husband, the baby in a stroller, and I were taking a stroll down a busy New Jersey street filled with people, stores, traffic, and the smell of amazing Latino food. He turned to me and said, "I don't feel good." Suddenly, he collapsed, saying, "My left leg isn't responding, and I don't feel my left arm. I can't get up." At this point, I didn't know what to think or do. I immediately went into survival mode, asking a stranger to stay with him while I went to get our car and put the baby in the car seat. I was confused, but with no time to really think about what was happening. He looked afraid, but calm, so I also tried to be calm and collected for his sake. Inside, I was thinking, *What is going on? Do I call his mother or do I call my mother first? Do I take him home or to a hospital?* I was young, I was naïve, and I was afraid!

We were able to see a neurologist, who, within two weeks, confirmed the diagnosis of multiple sclerosis. I had never even heard of it and didn't know anything about it. My husband, on the other hand, remembered hearing about it from an incident that had happened over two years earlier. He had lost the vision in his right eye, but tests were done and, at the time, multiple sclerosis was ruled out.

My rock bottom moment began here.

I was 20-years-old with an infant, married to a 26-year-old man just diagnosed with a terrible condition—a condition few knew about, had more questions than answers, and, more importantly, had no proven medications at the time. With the help of my sister-in-law, we got my husband accepted into a study program by a renowned neurologist in New York City. We didn't know whether the medication given in the study was a placebo or the real thing, but we were hopeful. We later found out the study was not successful and it was discontinued.

My mind started getting the best of me, and I began to imagine a very bleak future: me putting my dreams aside to take care of this man, perhaps not having any more children, or (God forbid) that our child may have been exposed to this dreaded disease.

Questions clouded my thoughts: Do I run or do I stay? If I cut my losses before he gets sicker, will I be viewed as a horrible person? What about the vows I made that included "in sickness and in health?" What about the life I imagined, the one with us in our eighties and traveling the world together and living out our dreams? Was God playing a joke on me? Was this a punishment for being a rebellious child to my parents? Did I not pray enough before getting married? Was this not the man for me? Did I move too fast and marry the first guy who proposed to me? Did I bring this upon myself? Are we going to live a sexless life? Am I going to have to become the sole breadwinner? And so on, and so on…

Now, not only did I feel terrible about the situation, but I also felt guilty for even thinking these thoughts. Who was I to question God, anyway?

Having grown in wisdom, I've not only learned that it's okay to question God and be honest with what I am facing, but that in our darkest hour, in our rock bottom moments, He welcomes us to run into His arms. I remember crying myself to sleep at night because I felt I couldn't share such horrible thoughts with anyone else. However, if we are not honest about how we feel, how can we expect others to help and bring hope? Putting on a façade that I was okay only hurt me and prevented me from receiving the proper assistance. I am still growing in the area of not holding back and requesting help when needed.

I have also learned that I serve a God of hope. In Genesis 8:1 (NIV), it states, "But God remembered Noah…and the flood began to disappear." My friend, God has not forgotten about you or your situation. We serve a God who loves and cares for His children.

My family and friends were also a great source of support. I am wired to be an independent woman, and I feared (and at times I even still fear) that people will view me as a weak woman if I ask for assistance. In my journey, I have learned that I must put down my pride and admit that I need help, even when that means physically moving over a thousand miles to be close to family.

I remember walking into my mother's home and being met by my grandmother's open arms. No words, just a hug that will stay with me forever. Although that hug took place over twenty years ago, I still hold it vividly in my mind. My grandmother is no longer with us, but her impact on my life will never be forgotten.

In January of 2013, God told me that my word for the year would be "embrace." I had never had a word to live by before, but I welcomed it. He also gave me Isaiah 61. I have been appointed to bring the good news of hope to the poor and the brokenhearted. I needed to embrace that calling on my life. Later that year, He told me I needed to embrace my voice, which is still something that I am learning to do. For 2014, He gave me the word "transformation." Through the transformation of my mind, I will be able to walk into everything that He has planned for me.

How am I doing today? How is my husband doing today? Well, we have three beautiful daughters and I am living out my dreams. With my husband, the truth is, there are good days and not-so-good days. However, we both know that he is a walking miracle. I am constantly reminded that God does love me and wraps His arms around me when I need it the most. We look forward to growing old together, traveling, and living out the rest of our dreams.

For me, my friend, rock bottom is a beautiful place—it's where I came to know that God picked me to be the wife to this amazing man and the mother to his amazing girls. God picked me for this very special assignment, and I wouldn't have it any other way.

Silvia is a Life Breakthrough Coach, board-certified biblical counselor, and the founder of Women's Empowerment Services. She is passionate about seeing women thrive, live out their destinies, and rekindle their dreams in a confident manner. Silvia lives in south Florida with her husband of twenty-five years and her three beautiful daughters. You can find out more about Silvia at www.womensempowermentservices.com.

Moving to Foreign Lands

"For I know the plans I have for you," declares the LORD, "plans to prosper you and not to harm you, plans to give you hope and a future." – Jeremiah 29:11 (NIV)

Dr. Michelle Bengtson

I was not unfamiliar with trials—I had had many during my childhood years. But now I was supposed to be living my happily ever after.

Or so I thought.

My husband and I met during my junior year of college and married a year later. I transitioned from having always lived with my parents and brother to getting married and living with my husband. I had never lived on my own. Those first few newlywed years were priceless…the calm before the storms.

A bachelor's degree in psychology doesn't prepare you to do much after graduation. Ever since I was very young, however, I knew I would go on for an advanced degree. I wanted to be in a position to support my family in case anything ever happened to my husband. Becoming a psychologist meant pursuing my doctorate, so after graduating with my bachelor's degree in psychology, that's what I set out to do. And God provided a way.

On Christmas Eve, my husband and I stood in the U.S. Post Office, mailing graduate school application after graduate school application, literally using all the coins left in our jar of collected spare change. We waited patiently (and sometimes less patiently), for the news of my graduate school acceptance to come.

I was finally accepted to a local program, which allowed me to study while he kept his job to support our family for the next several years. By this time we started receiving more jabs and jests from family and friends who wondered when we would add to the world's population by increasing our own family size. To their dismay, we delayed our family planning so that I could finish school.

Saying that those years were hard years is an understatement at the very least. The courses were demanding, the practicums were strenuous, and the constant feedback we students received was difficult to hear, but all designed to make us better clinicians. Deep in the recesses of my heart, when I remembered my motivation for pursuing my degree, I always knew the end result was worth it, but there were days when I would wonder. I excelled as a student—I knew how to study, I could write strong term papers, and I could deliver persuasive presentations. The hours were long, yet I had to keep the ultimate goal in mind and stay focused on my next immediate task, or else the stress could become unmanageable. Divorce rates are high among couples where one spouse is in graduate school, and we were well aware of those statistics.

Throughout my graduate training, my attention flitted between the current chapter to be read, the next paper to be written, my client load, or the final destination of having the degree and working in the field. I felt fairly comfortable with those daily to-dos, because to a large extent, accomplishing those tasks depended on me. If I did well on enough of those daily to-dos, they would naturally culminate in the resulting degree. Rarely, however, during those first couple of years did I think about the intermediate step: internship and "bloody Monday."

In order to earn our degree and become licensed in the field, we were required to complete a year of internship and then post-doctoral fellowship. Because

I specialized in my field, it necessitated that I apply to internships all over the country to increase the likelihood of getting a placement. On one designated Monday, not so fondly dubbed "bloody Monday," all prospective interns would find out whether or not they would "match" with an internship site. That was part of the process over which we had little to no control.

There was a very high likelihood that if I was going to continue to pursue the career I felt God had called me to, that it would require me to take an internship placement away from home, away from my husband, away from all things familiar and comfortable...including the security and approval of family and friends.

During the internship application process (yes, another round of applications and postage paid from our spare change jar!!), I sought the counsel and prayer of a very wise woman from my church. To this day I can't tell you what she told me. But one day prior to meeting with her to pray over our situation, I was a bit early so I wandered through the church bookstore. I glanced at a keychain hanging for sale next to the cash register, and it was as if the Lord had written me a personal letter on it that afternoon: "For I know the plans I have for you, declares the Lord. Plans to prosper you and not to harm you, plans for a future and a hope" (Jeremiah 29:11).

Where had that verse come from? I had memorized hundreds of verses up to that point in my life, but I couldn't recall having ever read that one before. That was the assurance that I needed. I didn't know what the future would hold, but God did. And no matter what it looked like to me, God would use it for good.

"Bloody Monday" came and went. The results were a Rock Bottom experience of sorts. While I was accepted into one of the top internship sites in the country in my area of specialization, an honor to be sure, it meant I would be leaving my husband, our extended families, our friends, our church (everything I knew and loved) for the unknown, the unfamiliar, the unpopular, and the frightening. This choice was not a popular decision within our families, and that added to the weightiness of the task. Yet we had prayed, and my husband and I were in agreement that this was what I needed to do and be faithful to God's leading.

It was frightening and it was exhilarating, all at the same time. I opened myself up to a great deal of criticism. I had to deal with my own insecurities of being "on my own." I had to depend on God in a much more active, much more constant day-by-day, moment-by-moment way than I ever had before. Even when others voiced their criticism, I had to remember God's promise for "plans to prosper you and not to harm you, plans for a future and a hope."

That was over twenty years ago, and as a result of God's faithfulness during that experience, I have clung to that verse so many more times when I have been unsure how my life circumstances were going to turn out. Now I'm much more at peace even in the not knowing…for it's enough to know I have a future and hope, which came out of a beautiful rock bottom place.

Dr. Michelle Bengtson has been a clinical neuropsychologist for over twenty years, and is passionate about affirming others' worth, encouraging their faith, and restoring their hope in the glory of God. She believes that without hope, we have nothing, but with Christ we always have hope. She speaks to groups about overcoming life's adversities. Dr. Bengtson has been married to God's gift to her for over twenty-five years and together, they have been blessed with two sons. www. DrMichelleBengtson.com

God and a Grandmother's Love

My grace is sufficient for you, for my power is made perfect in weakness.
– 2 Corinthians 12:9 (NIV)

Kathy B. Bornarth M.A., NCC, LPC

Love can heal in the darkest places. My "rock bottom" spanned what seemed to be a lifetime for someone so young. One month before my seventeenth birthday, I gave birth to my first child. By the time I was twenty-one, I had two children, got married and then divorced, found out I was adopted by my father, and became a single mother with no education, working as a part-time waitress and bartender.

I grew up in an alcoholic home. My dad (step-dad) was physically and verbally abusive to my mother and to my sisters and me. I remember spending most of my childhood in fear of what would happen next.

While most of my friends were having parties and friends over, I was too afraid to let anyone know what my household was like. I feared my parents would be fighting or dad would come home drunk in the middle of the night, so I rarely had my girlfriends sleep over. I spent most of my young life anxious or embarrassed.

By the time I hit my teen years, I started to become defiant. I was tired of living this way and tired of my mother not doing anything to make our situation better. When I was sixteen, I ran away from home with a guy I met at school. I was just looking for a way out and he was willing to go along with it. Not exactly the best decision to make, but when you're sixteen, you'll do whatever you need to do to get out of a bad situation, even if the new situation isn't much better.

Baby #1 arrived less than a year later.

With life not being much better, I left that relationship and was once again on a search for love. I was married to another man at age nineteen and had another child by twenty-one. Before my daughter was one, I was planning to divorce and move on.

What I didn't know then, but surely know now, is that you have to love yourself and know your value in Christ before you can truly love others.

Most days, I found myself lacking any motivation to change my circumstances. Depression and a sense of hopelessness had set in. It was difficult to get out of bed.

I could barely afford to take care of myself, let alone two young girls. Feeling desperate, I asked my grandmother if we could move in with her. Grammy, as our family called her, was always there for us when we were in trouble or needed support. She had plenty of room for the girls and me, and, since she was retired, she was able to help.

As I struggled to get my life back on track, Gram took care of my girls. She would walk my oldest to school and then come home to take care of my youngest. She helped them with schoolwork, fed all of us, and never complained.

With help from Gram and my Aunt Dottie, I was able to map out a plan for myself to go back to school, find a job that would fit my interests, and launch a career. These two great ladies also helped bring a relationship with the Lord into my life. They were both devout Catholics. Gram would pray for me and taught my girls to pray as well. My aunt would take me to her church in Allentown, Pennsylvania, where she participated in a charismatic small group. I enjoyed going with her, and I came to see God working in my life and healing my situation.

Finally, I was on a path to putting my life back together. Within a couple of years, I earned my bachelor's degree in psychology, moved into my own apartment, and found a job where I quickly advanced to management positions.

Gram continued to watch my girls when I worked. Money was always tight, so having her help kept my head above water. She never complained and, in fact, she loved us like no one ever had. Gram loved the Lord and showered that love on her granddaughter and great-grandchildren.

My healing and personal growth continued. I knew I had to leave my hometown and make a real life for myself so, after a few years on my own, I decided to move to Virginia. Although my family was sad to see us go, they knew I still needed to spread my wings and keep growing.

Within a year of moving to Virginia, I met my husband—the love of my life. We knew the moment we met that God had brought us together because we needed each other. We've been married now for twenty-four years.

Today, I'm a licensed professional counselor. I own and operate a counseling center in Chantilly, Virginia. As God redeemed me, He equipped me to offer His healing and love to others who so desperately need to know Him and His peace. My rock bottom taught me to trust God, to accept love and support from others, and to never give up on the plans God has for me.

I feel so blessed to have come through my wilderness with the help of a loving Christian grandmother. She never gave up on anyone, including me. Though Gram has been with the Lord for twelve years now, I'll never forget how she showed me God's love through her actions.

I pray for those of you reading this book to know God loves you unconditionally and will never give up on you. He can bring you out of the darkest places in your life and shower you with His light and love. Your pain and trials may challenge you, but you can draw strength and comfort from knowing they are also opportunities to draw closer to God.

Kathy Bornarth is owner and principal at Hope Counseling Center in Chantilly, Virginia. She has more than seventeen years of clinical experience as a therapist and has practiced throughout Pennsylvania, North Carolina, Florida, and Virginia. In addition to her counseling practice, Kathy is a national speaker, and teaches health and wellness seminars to Fortune 500 companies. Kathy holds a master of arts in counseling from Liberty University and a bachelor's degree in psychology from DeSales University. She is a licensed professional counselor, life coach, a member of the American Association of Christian Counselors, and a national certified counselor. She and her husband (retired Navy) have three grown children. They make their home in northern Virginia with their dog, Elvis. Kathy can be found at www. hccva.org, www.coachingbuffet.com, www.journaling4faith.com, and www.girlsandpearlsllc.com.

Loneliness Interrupted

"For I am about to do something new. See, I have already begun!....I will make a pathway through the wilderness. I will create rivers in the dry wasteland."
– Isaiah 43:19 (NLT)

Sabine Brandt

They say Christmas is one of the most difficult times of the year for divorcees, but what I experienced on December 25, 2006 was unlike anything I could have possibly imagined. It was on that day that Jesus met me at rock bottom, the place we find ourselves when we have exhausted all our resources and are left without any hope of escaping our present circumstances.

My two beautiful girls, six and eight at the time, had gone to spend the holiday with their dad, leaving me alone with my thoughts, my regrets, and my shortcomings—of which there had been many up to that point. I had struggled through a difficult marriage of ten years and a gut-wrenching divorce and custody battle that took several years, followed by the difficulties of single parenting, the near death of my youngest daughter, and several failed dating relationships.

Feelings of hopelessness, loneliness, shame, guilt, and unworthiness washed over me like a dark tide I couldn't hold back. I remember sitting in my empty house listening to the silence, and all I wanted was for the pain to stop, to not have to feel like this anymore, to forget my past, to start over, to feel loved and wanted again. It seemed that everything I had tried in my own strength utterly failed to bring me happiness. Even those I had considered my closest friends had abandoned me to focus on their own lives rather than hear yet another sob story about my broken heart.

Not wanting to sit at home alone, I decided to go to the movies by myself and watch the newly released movie, *The Nativity Story*. Little did I know, God was about to use this story to capture my heart and turn my life around. I don't know if it was the soundtrack (which included songs like "Breath Of Heaven" and "Mary, Did You Know?") or Joseph's utter devotion to Mary that got the best of me, but I do remember coming home and collapsing onto the floor where I lay face down, weeping for hours.

Although I was not unfamiliar with the gospel message, it was there that I really met Jesus for the first time. At this bittersweet place called "rock bottom," I laid down my life at His beautiful feet. I let Him comfort me and tell me everything would be okay. Along with my failed marriage and dating relationships, I handed over issues of self-worth, every critical word that had been spoken over me, and a whole truckload of "should haves."

From this point forward, I vowed not to make another move unless He directed it. Clearly, I had already demonstrated over and over again that I was not able to "do life" (let alone relationships) on my own, so handing over the wheel at this point felt like a huge weight lifted off my shoulders. I stopped dating completely and started going to church.

I remember walking into that church for the very first time, sensing the enemy's disapproval, and feeling like all eyes were on me, the divorcee and prodigal daughter. You see, I had always been a very private person, rarely leaning on others for support or letting others know what was going on in my life. I hated vulnerability and feared not being in control, so the possibility that someone would ask me about my situation and I would burst out in tears absolutely terrified me. Not only that, but most of my family and many of my friends were not too fond of my newfound spiritual life and didn't exactly encourage my pursuit. It was the grace of God and what seemed to be an unquenchable thirst for the living water Jesus offers that kept me going back weekend after weekend.

Not only did I want to learn God's way of doing relationships, I also wanted to know the truth about who I really was and why I was here. I soaked up God's Word like a sponge after all other spiritual teachings I had pursued in the past had turned out to be misleading half-truths and left my soul wanting more.

Over time, Jesus and I became best friends, and life gradually started feeling good again. The loneliness had been interrupted by a love far greater than any I had ever experienced. I was prepared to do anything for the hope He filled me with. As a result, I purged my home and life of anything that competed with His plan for me, including certain books on spirituality and dating that didn't agree with God's Word, and even certain people who threatened to draw me back into darkness. In other words, I quit trying to conjure up a happy life via the law of attraction, consulting with psychics, my horoscope, or Tarot cards, and instead, placed my destiny in the hands of the One who designed it.

Jesus prepared my heart to love again and allow myself to be loved. About one year later, I met my future husband—at church! I had just given my testimony, and he approached me after the service to introduce himself. A few weeks later, we met for lunch. By spring of the following year, we were married. God had kept His promise that if I let Him direct my steps, He would not fail me.

My rock bottom experience has transformed me in ways that are hard to describe in mere words. It has completely shifted my perspective on life and how I approach not only my relationships, but also my work, making me a better leader, parent, friend, and person.

Certainly life will continue to challenge me with its trials, but I know beyond the shadow of a doubt that whatever struggle may come, Jesus will always be the rock I can firmly stand on when the tide rises and waves of change crash wildly around me.

Sabine Brandt is president of Nobility Coaching and Consulting, Inc., and a certified business expert with nearly two decades of experience as an entrepreneur and corporate leader. Sabine delights in teaching her clients at www.nobilitycoaching.com how to create small businesses that not only provide financial freedom, but also a deep fulfillment of serving others and contributing to God's greater plan. In addition, Sabine serves as an executive coach and consultant to large organizations that wish to improve their operational processes and enhance their leadership capabilities.

Joy Comes In the Morning

Weeping may endure for a night, but joy comes in the morning. – Psalm 30:5 (KJ21)

Jessica Brassington

How did I get here? I asked myself, huddled in the fetal position and staring blankly at the walls of my childhood bedroom. The unnerving sound of my baby crying at the top of her lungs pushed down on me from all sides. *Is this real? It can't be real.* I was the first to graduate from college in my family. I had a good job. *This doesn't happen to people like me—maybe to the dropouts or teen moms you see on television, but not to me!*

Two years earlier, I had been a recent college graduate with my own apartment, car, and job. I thought I had it all figured out. Sure, I had slipped away from God, no longer attended church regularly, and now justified the boundary of sex outside of marriage, but I was a *good person*. I loved my family, helped my neighbors, and even volunteered. I prayed and read my Bible every now and then when I had a moment to spare. I was a busy lady!

Looking back, I realize that my relationship with God was like the seed that fell on shallow ground that Jesus spoke about. It began when a family friend invited me to church and I fell in love with the warmth and acceptance I felt there. I received salvation in seventh grade and was baptized. I constantly begged my parents to come to church with me, and they eventually did and became very involved with the children's program. Life seemed great and all was well with the world. As a child, I played the part to a T. I joined youth groups and held leadership positions. I attended camps and church whenever the doors were open. From the outside looking in, I had it all together and was a *good kid*: no cussing, drugs, or drinking—just a normal Christian teenager.

I had good intentions, but when my father died my freshman year of college, all of that went out the window. He was the glue that held my family together. Without our fearless leader, we were vulnerable and our tightknit unit fell apart. When I was left on my own in college, had more freedom, and faced hardship with my dad dying, I abandoned my faith and it slipped away. I know now that our source and strength *has* to come from our Heavenly Father, because this earth shall pass away like the people who inhabit it. Parents are sinners and make mistakes; they are loaned to us for a time, but God will never leave us nor forsake us.

Anger and confusion set in, and, instead of leaning on Him during this time, I turned to my boyfriend. Hoping to fill the ever-growing void in my heart, I focused on any distraction I could to take my attention away from the gnawing conviction I felt deep in the pit of my stomach that I needed to repent and give my life back to Christ.

Are you a businesswoman looking for a safe place to connect with fellow sisters of faith who understand the obstacles and challenges you face on a daily basis? Visit www.nacwe.org and discover the rich network of friends and resources that are available to you.

I broke off this relationship one year after graduating high school and left for Texas A&M University. I just *knew* this would be the start to something better in my life. My youth pastor encouraged me to join the Christian groups at school, but I didn't. Instead, I began going to parties and trying alcohol, thinking, *Isn't this what all college kids do?* I was never a big drinker, but one party led to another. The next thing I knew, that was my weekend agenda, along with showing up late for class the next Monday, fragrant with the unappetizing aroma of tequila.

After two years at the university, I moved to a different city to follow my boyfriend of barely a year. I'd come so far from the bright-eyed, ambitious girl whose father believed in her and told her she could do anything and make a difference in the world. You guessed it—it was not a fairy-tale romance and no happy ending ensued. Things fizzled out with him and I was now in a place with no family.

I soon entered into a new relationship. This was it. I convinced myself that I could change this one and show him what a great catch I was. I imagined him giving me that look my dad used to give me, a look that radiated love and acceptance, speaking without saying a word. Wrong again. Doomed from the beginning, it ended years later.

Since leaving my home as a teen, I had never connected with a church or rekindled my relationship with God. I worked out *a lot.* I entered beauty pageants and won several titles, all while lacking the feeling of complete self-worth I so desperately craved. I graduated from college and began working. One day at work, I met a guy. Even though I knew it wasn't the relationship God had in store for me (he was ending a relationship with the mother of his young son), I decided to try it. *How bad can it be?* I wondered. I eventually found out just how lost you can become when you take a detour from God's plan.

Mediocre turned into not so great, which gave way to undeniably ugly. He spent late nights out while I cared for his son, had continual hang-ups, and nights alone rapidly became the norm for me. I became pregnant and gave birth to a beautiful baby girl. Our eyes met and I was completely and utterly in L-O-V-E, love.

Now I was a mom and really wanted to make things work with her father. I sincerely believed things would change. They didn't. Ten months later, I decided that the third attempt to leave him would be my last. I couldn't take the lying, cheating, or drugs one more day. I purchased a one-way ticket to Houston for my best friend's housewarming party with no intentions of returning. Possessing only my daughter, her stroller, a diaper bag, a suitcase, and fifty dollars in cash, I left and didn't look back.

I returned to my mom's house and found myself unable to look into a mirror or face the day. I hated what I saw: a single mom with a baby girl, broke, skinny, stressed, heartbroken, and ashamed. What I thought was depression at the time gave way to morning sickness, unending nausea, and a constant Wicked-Witch-of-the-West hue of green. *Is it possible? It can't be!*

A visit to the doctor confirmed my worst nightmare: I was pregnant. Vast helplessness consumed every inch of my being and I sank into a deep mental abyss of overwhelming disbelief. At that very moment, I hit my rock bottom.

In destitution and desperation, I contemplated abortion. I decided to kill this life inside my womb. I was pro-life in theory and debates, but now that *I* was the one in the situation, it was a viable option and all previous discussions on life beginning at conception were a fleeting memory. I called the father and begged for money to cover the cost, but he cursed and denied my request. Thank God he did!

I sobbed and shook uncontrollably, half due to the fact that I had no clue where to go from there and the other half due to the shame I felt for even considering the abortion at all.

At that moment, I surrendered my life to Christ and asked Him to take control. I finally figured out that I didn't know the answers and couldn't do this on my own. My mom was so supportive, and I began going to church and surrounding myself with prayer warriors. It was *not* easy, but I knew God would replace what Satan had stolen from me if I followed Him. He not only replaced what I lost, but also blessed me beyond measure with a wonderful husband, gorgeous and healthy girls, and a whole new life.

I have learned from my rock bottom how totally dependent I am upon My Lord and Savior for all aspects of life. He is so good and faithful to forgive us and walk with us step by step. His ways are not my ways and I need to trust that He knows what is best for my life.

Rock bottom is a beautiful place because, when you hit it, there's no way but up. It is the ultimate region of brokenness and complete reliance on God our Father. His love, grace, and forgiveness exude beauty in this place.

Jessica Brassington is a Texas wife and homeschool mom to three girls. She is a writer, blogger, speaker, and mommy mentor. Her passion for inspiring and encouraging other moms to live life to the fullest is matched only by her love for her family and friends. Find out more about Jessica and her ministry at www.mykalekids.com.

ROCK BOTTOM IS A BEAUTIFUL PLACE

Rock Bottom Cannot Be a Beautiful Place Without God

God chose what the world considers weak to shame the strong.
— 1 Corinthians 1:27

Elizabeth Buhrke

Rock bottom cannot be a beautiful place without God, and I know He has met me in that valley place more than once.

Looking back, my first rock bottom would have been at the end of my seventh grade year. I emptied every pill bottle in our family medicine cabinet, intending to take them all. I closed the mirrored cabinet door to see my own reflection, but I didn't recognize the eyes looking back at me. These unfamiliar eyes talked me out of ending my life that night, and I found myself putting all of the pills back in their perspective bottles and returning them to the cabinet. However, I wouldn't recognize this as a rock bottom for years.

I was in college before it was pointed out to me, in counseling, that God had never abandoned me when I thought He was nowhere to be found. It has taken me years to recognize the lies of the enemy, those whispers that told me that God had left me hanging as a young child in that classroom for those boys to sexually abuse during recess, or that He was not around on the track and field overnight trip in seventh grade when I was raped in the hotel stairwell by one of those same boys from elementary school. The truth is, God cried during each and every one of those moments. He was crying when I was too numb to even try.

A runner by nature, I have loved being active since I can remember, and I played competitive sports into college. However, running is how I dealt with life too. I ran to eating disorders beginning in middle or high school to keep myself numb from having to deal with the past. When I could no longer control things, I ran between anorexia and bulimia throughout the rest of high school. It was scripture about treating my body as a temple of God that led me to getting help between high school and college. It took all summer to train my body to accept food again.

It wasn't until I was willing to face the pain of the brutal attack that occurred on that cold dark night my freshman year of college before I began to see God in it all. I chose to walk down a street in the middle of the night that I knew wasn't safe to even drive down in the middle of the day. God spared my life that night, but not before being raped by some strange man in a vacant lot where a church now stands (talk about redemption!).

It seemed like this man was on top of me forever and yet, it all ended so abruptly. I thought I would die that night. I've wished many days since then that I had, but God had other plans that wouldn't make sense until years later. I truly believe God removed this stranger from on top of me. It is the only way to explain why he didn't kill me. He was way too big for me to have gotten away any other way.

It wouldn't be until five years later that I would be able to make sense out of why I became pregnant from such brutal circumstances though. I had to stand up to doctors and rape crisis counselors to not end the life of that child growing inside me, regardless of whether she was created from a loving relationship or not. While I prayed endlessly for God to take care of the situation, I was left feeling regret for those prayers when I lost the baby the night before I went to fill out the paperwork to put her up for adoption. I would use the same questions I asked myself during this process a few years later when I became pregnant outside of the covenant of marriage. While I know God is not happy about the sins we commit, I am convinced that first He saved me through sending His son to die on the cross to forgive my sin. Then He saved me from myself by sending me my son.

Growing up the oldest daughter of a pastor, I didn't expect the response of loving parents coming along side me during this time to support me in any of this, but God had just prepared them by having them walk their best friends through a similar situation. I had just graduated college a few months earlier. I had left my job to pursue life on the road as a Christian musician, so not only did I not have stable income, I was also living out of my car with no real place to call home. While I loved the life, it was not any way to live with a baby. I gave up my dreams of becoming the next Amy Grant, and found a job and a place to live.

Four days after my son was born, a very routine pediatrician's visit turned into a whirlwind of additional appointments that same afternoon. There was something wrong with his eyes. The doctors initially diagnosed him with retinal blastoma, a childhood cancer of the eye. We were advised to go to Children's Chicago immediately for further testing and to begin chemotherapy. Appointments were made for the next day in Chicago while additional tests were scheduled in town that night.

He was baptized in our kitchen early that morning before heading to Chicago. They wanted to do an ultrasound of the eye, test for cancer through his soft spot, do a spinal tap, and put the port in to start chemo immediately. I went from wondering how I was going to provide for us to fearing how little time he was going to be a part of my life.

It would quickly be determined that it was not cancer, but because he had a very rare genetic disease, he would not have much chance of regaining his sight. Like being a single mom wasn't rock bottom enough, all of a sudden I became a single mom of a blind child. In kindergarten we added mild hearing loss to his diagnosis, and I became a single mom of a deaf/blind child. In first grade we spent a year or two determining whether his many broken legs were an additional part of the disease or just the result of an active young boy.

In third grade he would lose additional hearing, which gave him moderate loss in one ear. There was a drastic change in his hearing again in the sixth grade that would raise him to 70 percent loss in each ear overnight. We had completed two cycles of testing by then to determine whether we were dealing with any type of autism as well.

Growing up, I had numbed myself with eating disorders and busyness. When I became pregnant from the assault in college, I turned to gangs. They gave me my first sense of belonging, but added to the pain I carried. As an adult, I chose to run to drugs and alcohol, and don't remember much of my son's toddler years. He received amazing services that have been an integral part in giving him a strong basis in which to remain grade level today. God's hand has not left me, and He has had a plan in all of it, just as Jeremiah talks about in the Old Testament.

My son is a happy and healthy teenager who just happens to not see with his eyes like you or I and has trouble hearing clearly, but he still has perfect pitch and often asks why a familiar song is being done in a different key during worship. Like any teenager, he has chores around the house and has interests in girls.

His greatest gift is that he has taught me how to experience life for the first time. I went from my own deathbed, spending three months in the hospital because of internal organs shutting down due to eating disorders, to God entrusting me to carry a life into this world. I was able to eat for him, which taught me how to eat for myself. I couldn't get clean and sober for myself, but could for him until I learned to do it for myself. God provided a church family to love both of us unconditionally and for me to be able to walk into the healing God has always had for me. And now we both are involved in serving God the best way we know how, with the gifts He has given us.

Each of us have rock bottom experiences individual to us. While some of us can pinpoint one specific rock bottom, others of us have several to choose from.

My rock bottom story seems to be a collection of a variety of events, but each is an integral part of what God has done in my life and what has brought me to where I am today.

Elizabeth Buhrke is a Mary Kay consultant, Beachbody coach, data analyst, and single mother of a deaf/blind/autistic 14-year-old son. A worship leader at heart, she has just recently returned to speaking and sharing what God has done in her life after a ten year hiatus. Elizabeth's passion for the Lord compels her to share, through word and song, the dark places from which Christ has drawn her. Her foundational joy is rooted in Christ and reflected brightly in the life of her son. She counts them both as integral reasons she is alive and empowered to share the gospel with others today.

ROCK BOTTOM IS A BEAUTIFUL PLACE

Surrendering to Joy

Don't ask what the world needs. Ask what makes you come alive, and go do it.
Because what the world needs is people who have come alive.
– Howard Thurman

Tina Cochran

Sometimes rock bottom comes with a crash and the trauma of your life falling apart. It's large, noisy, and messy. But sometimes rock bottom arrives as a simple statement that makes you realize things can no longer stay the way they are. I had lived with chaos and drama for so long it seemed normal. It took one powerful comment from my son to show me I had reached rock bottom.

My son Anthony has autism and as such, being tactful is not always his best skill. In the fall of 2008, then 10 years old, he looked at me and said "Mommy, you need to go on *The Biggest Loser.*" The words hit me hard with a realization that he was worried about me and knew I needed to change. The over 250 pounds I was carrying on my 5 ft. 4 in. frame was no longer something I could ignore or hide.

At his insistence, the NBC show, *The Biggest Loser,* became part of our weekly schedule. Every week he would watch the show and I would hide my tears as I sunk deep into the hopelessness of obesity and the over-scheduled life I was living. I continued to make excuses and justifications why I couldn't do anything about my weight. His direct comment crashed into those excuses and held them against rock bottom. I began to realize that I was no longer going to be able to ignore or hide from an attempt to do something.

In November of 2008, I started a weight loss program. The plan was simple—I would try this "diet" for a week or so and when it didn't work, I would then focus on finding a way to convince myself and my son that my body would always be this way, and it really wasn't a problem.

I am grateful to report that I was wrong and God used this program to help me lose over 100 pounds and keep it off. What started out as a solution to accepting that things would never change actually became a catalyst for a change I never imagined.

Over the past few years, I have learned the truth of who I am. As the pounds melted away, a woman I didn't know began to appear. This woman was strong and confident in her worth and had a heart to serve. Eventually I joined the company that designed my weight loss program and became a certified health coach.

By telling this story, my fear is that you will see it as another weight loss success story and miss the real transformation. While hitting rock bottom regarding my weight began my journey, it is actually not the most important change that has happened for me. When I was released from my corporate job in July 2009, I became a full-time coach. At the time I thought my journey was complete. I believed I had built myself up from the depths of obesity, stress, and depression to health, peace, and happiness.

What I didn't realize was that joy was waiting around the next corner, and it would require another visit to rock bottom. At first life was happy and exciting. But eventually I developed an obsession with business and marketing that drove me to work endless hours, never enjoying life or my family. I was constantly chasing better ways to make more money and grow my business. Founding a nonprofit organization only added to the stress and anxiety I felt every day. My relationship with my family suffered (especially my husband), and I woke up every day in a state of panic. While I was keeping my body a size eight and telling the world I was at peace and happy, in my heart I knew it was a lie.

I felt like a fraud.

The strength and confidence I found during my weight loss journey eroded until I found myself once again feeling hopeless to change. I was actually living at rock bottom, just in a prettier package. It took a tornado to break my heart wide open and motivate me to change. I live near Joplin, Missouri. In May of 2011, an F-5 tornado tore the town to pieces. I followed the destruction on social media and my heart broke more with every passing day. God had given me a gift of empathy and my heart filled to capacity with the pain around me. In my personal life, the stress of chasing my business, building a nonprofit, and pleasing my family became overwhelming. I spent many days and nights in tears, begging God to take my life and bring me home. On the outside my life looked like it was growing and becoming more successful every day. However, inside I was dying and falling apart.

For the next six months, I struggled to find a solution, something that would make the pain go away. Finally I ran out of strength to search and collapsed in despair. It was only then that I heard the still, small voice. "Stop studying business and study Me." God's voice was quiet, but insistent. It brought my spinning mind to a halt.

"But how will I make a living, God?" I asked. "You won't. You will make a life," was the only answer He would give. "Get to know Me, who I am, and who I created you to be. Bring all your focus and energy on searching for Me. When you find Me, you will find all that you need. Trust Me, I will provide. I created you for a very special purpose. It's time for you to be set apart and learn all I have to teach you."

With much fear and trembling, I put my business books away and opened my Bible. I began a search for who God was and what He wanted from me. This search led me to a life I never could have imagined. It has also led me through periods of brokenness I never would have chosen. The pain of coming face to face with the mistakes of my past choices and the things I have done that have not honored my loving Father have been beyond anything I thought I could survive. Through it all, God has gently and lovingly held my hand and reminded me that His plans for me are good. It has not always been pretty and it has never been easy, but it has been worth it. Not only have I survived, I have begun to thrive.

Rock bottom is a beautiful place. I know this beyond a shadow of a doubt because rock bottom is the place where you find the strength to surrender yourself completely to the One who created you. It's not until you come completely to the end of yourself that you can truly begin to live. The most beautiful part is that by creating a life with rock bottom as the foundation, you find true joy.

Tina Cochran (aka, The Joy Architect) is a woman on a mission. She is driven to empower women to design a life of Joy that fits. Her Empowered Alignment™ approach in coaching and consulting combines tools with action plans that lead women to create lives of strength, confidence, and purpose. As an obesity survivor, she uses her own journey from survival mode to Joy to inspire and motivate others. A gifted writer and speaker, she offers her insights with humor, heart, and honesty. She lives her life of Joy with her husband and son on a 25-acre alpaca ranch in Adrian, Missouri. http://www.TinaCochran.com

Ashes to Beauty

Jessica Daley

I was sitting in the airport after the NACWE 2014 Catch on Fire conference. The women in attendance introduced me to new concepts: "Your soul is not your business, and your soul is your business. Be real. Allow your pain to catapult your business." The knowledge I took away from the conference was astounding, tangible, and holistic for the mind, body, and soul.

We were told of an opportunity to be contributing authors for this book. The idea of being a published author sounded attractive to me, and I had already divulged my story to the group. "Sure," I thought to myself. "This could help me in my business." I guess I had already forgotten the holistic approach: it could be healing for my soul, too.

I had planned on using the time on the plane ride home back to Fort Collins, Colorado to create my new webinar, "Take Your Fear Out of Your Finances." However, in my spirit I heard God whisper, "I will write your webinar; you write your story." The business side comes easy to me, but I knew I needed to engage in the hard part: creating. God met me on that plane in a real way. He not only asked me to share my story with you, but also to realize that my brokenness in this area was hindering my growth. My story and my business needed to converge into one entity.

I cried the entire plane ride home, especially when I read Cheryl Cresswell's "Evidence of Divine Inspiration" from *Inspired Women Succeed*. She mentioned Isaiah 61:3, which says, "To all who mourn he will give a crown of beauty for ashes." Cheryl wrote, "I discovered how my skills, experience, and passions would come together to give me a beautiful assignment. Are you mourning over the ashes found in heartache when God is ready to give you beauty?" I was ready to let God turn my ashes into a beautiful assignment.

Ever since I was a little girl, I wanted four children. The number never scared me; I welcomed the challenge. I married a great man in 2000, and we began our journey together. I remember a distinct conversation with my husband. He mentioned his desire for adoption, but I quickly shut down that idea with a "four of my own children" comment. We moved from South Carolina to Washington to plant a church in the least churched city in the U.S. at the time—Seattle.

In 2004 it was time to start a family, and it didn't take long. Our son, Jude, was born in February of 2005. I assumed it would always be that easy. However, in March of 2006, I began having shoulder pain and couldn't breathe when I lay down. Twenty-four hours later, I was in the operating room as the surgeons removed a tubal pregnancy that had blown out of my fallopian tube. Thankfully, my tubes were spared and, since I did not even know I was pregnant, the emotional pain was minimal. In August of 2006, I became

---

Are you walking through your own Rock Bottom and need some encouragement and support? Visit

www.rockbottomisabeautifulplace.com/freegift

and download our FREE GIFT to you.

pregnant a third time. However, I sensed when my hunger ceased that something was not right. The doctor confirmed eight weeks later…a blighted ovum. Four weeks after the doctor's visit, that baby went to Jesus as I sat in the bathroom and let him or her go.

I had the most difficult time as I watched my friend's children being born around the same time mine would have been. I would drop Jude off in the nursery at church and see the ages Jude's siblings would have been. It was devastating. I was a pastor's wife at the time and these moms were my flock. Yet, I struggled with jealousy and discontentment in my heart. My desire was staring me in the face and emotions would flood to the surface at the most inopportune times. Was it discontentment or pure grief and loss? I think it was both. I hit rock bottom. My hormones couldn't figure out what to do, and I was depressed. I needed more sleep. Meanwhile, I had Jude to care for (whose name means "may God be praised.")

In April of 2007, I became pregnant for the fourth time, this time getting more positive signs as the doctors relayed it would be a "viable pregnancy." I remember using that word with such excitement. Twelve weeks later, I asked my husband to stay home from an elder meeting as I shook and trembled during a mini-labor once again. He stood by my side as this baby also went to see Jesus. I went to bed, cried, and fell asleep. I received flowers from one of the elders and his wife that said, "You are still a good mother." Little did they know those words would comfort me even to this day.

Over the next two years, as I wrestled with God, my emotions, and my desires, I found myself hearing internal lies like, "God doesn't think you can handle more than one," or, "If you were a better mother, God would give you more." My emotional grief was too much for me and those around me. However, it wasn't too much for God. I read the Psalms, even though I felt like I was just reading words on a page. God spoke to me, even though I didn't sense it or feel it. Our sweet Jude was four years old, and I praised God for my precious boy. My grief started turning away from me and towards his future grief of having no siblings. My husband and I had siblings, and we knew the bond he was missing. Each birthday that would roll around expressed the sadness in our hearts, for us and Jude.

After the third loss, God began working in my heart towards adoption. After much training and prayer, our life was interrupted by a six-week-old, drug-exposed infant through the state's foster-to-adopt program. Six months later, we also took in a seventeen-month-old boy. I had Jude and two in diapers—overwhelming, challenging, and satisfying all at once. However, both sets of birthparents began to make better choices, become more stable, and were able to get their children back. I was devastated again. Now I believed even deeper internal lies: "You're not even good enough for the state foster care system. Why do you even think you can be a 'mother of many?'" However, it wasn't about me, even in those moments of loss. It was about my calling to a world around me. There will be pain in this world that we cannot escape until we see Jesus. It was not my fault. Some of you reading this may also need to hear "It's not your fault." It is part of the broken world we live in that God will someday restore. My hope is still that God will fill our table with children; we tangibly believed that as we purchased a beautiful table off of Craigslist that can seat up to twelve. As the three of us eat our meals around it, we are reminded of our hope.

We moved to Colorado after the second foster child went to live with his birth mom. God gave us grace with the timing, as He was calling us to other entrepreneurial ventures. The night his foster brother left, Jude said, "Is he going to forget my name?" We were brokenhearted, individually and collectively, as a family.

After living in Colorado for six months, international adoption seemed to be the route God was asking of us. However, the expenses were the cost of a down payment on a house. We had seen God's mighty provision over the years and knew if this was of Him, He would provide again. I started Xcelerate Business Solutions, a finance company specializing in educating women in business and offering services such as bookkeeping, payroll, and budgeting. Within a year, we had $10,000 saved for adoption costs, along with a large $24,000 donation that gave us more than what we needed. The extravagance of this donation overwhelmed us with God's love and support of our risky endeavors. My business took off and working part-time, I made way more than I even hoped. I took off the LLC and became incorporated, as I was growing and could see God's hand in my company.

The Friday before Mother's Day 2012, I sat down to read the Bible. I prayed God would speak to me with the first thing I read. I opened my Bible and four Psalms were staring at me. I chose to read Psalm 113. I could not believe how up close and personal God spoke to me and my fears. Psalm 113:7-9 (NIV) says, "He raises the poor from the dust and lifts the needy from the ash heap. He seats them with princes, with the princes of his people. He settles the childless woman in her home as a happy mother of children. Praise the Lord." I knew in that moment and still cling to it today—God comforts my pain, turns our ashes to beauty, will raise the needy from ashes to sit at my table, and will let me be a mother of children. Throughout this season of growth in our lives, we have had multiple opportunities to minister to many families who struggle with the same issues.

This pain has begun to turn my ashes to beauty as we hope to start Xcelerate Family Foundation, a non-profit linked to my business, offering infertility counseling for women and adoption funds to fill their families. Our ability to engage in our own grief and loss will allow me to engage in others' loss and, hopefully someday, my adopted children's losses. Where are we now? We are still waiting. Will I forever want more biological children? Yes. Will our future adopted children forever want their biological parents? Yes. That's why adoption is beautiful. God uses you to fill that void along with His spirit that lives within us.

God adopted us. We adopt others.

Jessica Daley is the founder and director of Xcelerate Business Solutions. She is passionate about educating women in business, managing women's finances, and empowering women's decision-making skills. Jessica has always enjoyed budgeting, mastering good deals, and organizing financial chaos. Jessica lives with her family, a very supportive husband and one son. To connect with Jessica, visit xcelerate-solutions.com.

ROCK BOTTOM IS A BEAUTIFUL PLACE

Consider It Joy

Dear brothers and sisters, when troubles come your way, consider it an opportunity for great joy. For you know that when your faith is tested, your endurance has a chance to grow. So let it grow, for when your endurance is fully developed, you will be perfect and complete, needing nothing.
– James 1:2-4 (NLT)

Tina Drake-Parmigiano

Over the course of the last thirty-five years, my life has hit "Rock Bottom" many times. I was raised a preacher's daughter in a small town called Halfway, Oregon that boasted a population of 360 people. I always knew who Jesus was, that He had died on the cross for me, and had taken away my sins. I knew that He loved me and no matter what, He would never leave me.

But that wasn't the problem. The problem was, I kept leaving Him.

Through the years, I would go back and forth, drinking and doing a few drugs here and there. When I was twenty-two, I joined the Air Force, only to be discharged with an early separation status because I was pregnant. I moved back home with my parents and within the next year, my father was diagnosed with cancer and passed away three weeks before my son's first birthday.

Boy did that set me on a whirlwind of blaming God for everything. I was so angry! I turned and ran away from God again, hiding behind the bottle, hanging with friends, and neglecting my son. It took moving 3000 miles away to get a grip on myself and to get my life back on track as a mother. However, I never fully turned back to God. Oh, I knew He was there, and I prayed and went through the actions and talk, but I never really gave Him my heart.

After a year went by, things did not work out for me on the West Coast, so I moved back to the East Coast. Two months later, my sister set me up on a blind date, and he turned out to be the man I was going to marry only eleven months later. My son was now four and he finally had a man in his life.

Over the next ten years or so, "Rock Bottom" came and stayed awhile. Our next son was born and at eighteen months old, he developed some medical issues that kept me from going back to work. We went through bankruptcy. I became a stay-at-home mom and had a third son, and four years later, along came our fourth son. We lived in a 14' x 70' mobile home on a Navy base, and things were tight in that little mobile home. (There's nothing like togetherness!)

It was there I started doing taxes at home for some extra income. Soon after the birth of our fourth son, my husband received a promotion and we were able to move into a new home big enough for all of us. Things were going well…or so I thought. You see, I was doing things my way. I went to church on and off, read my Bible here and there, and of course, I always prayed when I needed something. After all, that was what God was there for, right?

Well, life took a turn again. My sister was diagnosed with cancer for the third time. She had beat it twice before—but this time, it didn't look like she was going to pull through. My husband was transferred to a new duty station and we lost a large amount of monthly income because the housing allowance left when he did. Our bills had increased a great deal due to the new house and to top it off, he needed a new car. Could things get any worse?

I got back into church and really started getting involved. I started singing on the worship team (which was a dream of mine, since I had grown up singing), and I got involved in women's ministries. My sons started going to church with me, and I thought I had really become grounded in the Lord.

My sister ended up passing away at the age of forty-three from the cancer, and it took a lot out of me. You see, we had only become friends again over the previous several years, and I was really going to miss her. We wasted a lot of years on petty differences. She left a daughter who was in her early twenties, and I promised my sister I would take care of her whenever she needed me. That led to new trials that would enter my life.

Soon, I started straying down my own path again. My husband, not being a Christian, made it easier for me to just go with the flow. I would use that as an excuse to stop doing things. He never kept me from going to church or being involved, but things happened in the church and people left. Instead of hanging on to God, I just let one day lead into the other, and He was put on the back burner. That's when I started having problems with my oldest son.

He started hanging out with the wrong crowd and he was quickly heading down the path of destruction—a mother's worst nightmare. On the eve of his seventeenth birthday, he was in a motorcycle accident. Half of the lower right side of his face was torn off as he went face-first through the rear windshield of a parked van. He broke his upper jaw and had tons of cuts on his back and chest. He stayed in the trauma ICU for several days and underwent surgery before finally coming home. That event did not keep him from continuing down that same path. Things got much worse before they started getting better. He is now twenty-seven with three children of his own, and my other sons are now twenty-one, nineteen, and fifteen. There have been many more events that have been hard for me as a mother to endure, but God has pulled me through.

This past year, my father-in-law was diagnosed with stage-four cancer. It has brought back many memories of the past with my own father and sister. But this is when I found the beauty in Rock Bottom. It was a couple of months before my fiftieth birthday and things started to change. I got back into church, I got back into His Word, and for the first time in a very long time, I opened not only my mind, but also my heart and soul for the Lord to enter into.

You see, as I look back on all my experiences (and these few have only scratched the surface), I can see how God was always there. He had never left me nor forsaken me. He was right there waiting for me to cry out and reach for Him. I have learned to keep moving forward, to never give up hope. To forgive and love when I just didn't think it could be possible. I have found that no matter what I have ever done, no matter what I am going through, Jesus loves me unconditionally and His grace and mercies are new every morning when I get up. Always forgiving and always there to show me the way.

By telling you my story, I want you to understand and know that no matter what your situation is, it is never too big for God, but it is definitely too big for you to handle alone. Don't push Him away and try to deal with it on your own. God is just waiting to pour out His mercy and grace on you, to forgive you of anything and everything you have ever done or ever will do.

Now, when circumstances arise and I am faced with trials and tribulations, I am learning, as it says in James 1:2, to count it all joy when I fall into various trials. The joy is not found in the trial itself, but in leaning into God, searching and finding Him in the midst of it all, and all the while growing in our faith in Him. Put your trust in Him and in Him alone. He will never leave you nor forsake you. Who else do you know that would send His own son to die on a cross to take the blame for the sins of us all—past, present, and future?

Tina Drake-Parmigiano has been happily married for the past twenty-three years to her husband Mike. She is the mother of four sons and has two granddaughters and a grandson. She is the owner of a small tax practice, and is a Business Success Coach and mentor. Tina is passionate about sharing the love of the Lord and all He's doing in her life with other women. Encouraging them to never give up on themselves, to pursue a relationship with the only One who can truly change their life around. And, that no matter what life trials they have gone through or are going through, it's only temporary, and that the God of ALL Creation is right there and as you lean into Him, letting Him take full control, you too can consider it ALL Joy! Visit Tina at www.yourpathchristianlifecoaching. com

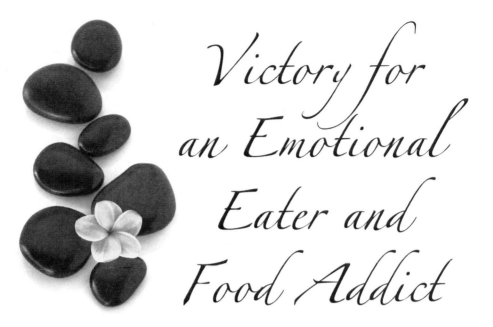

Victory for an Emotional Eater and Food Addict

Therefore, if anyone is in Christ, he is a new creation. The old has passed away; behold, the new has come. – 2 Corinthians 5:17 (ESV)

Ginny Edwards

Somewhere along the way, the belief that "I'm not good enough" attached itself to me like a cancerous growth. This belief affected everything I did, including my hundreds of attempts to create the perfect body. The power of this limiting belief was astounding as it even impacted the relationships I attracted into my life—relationships that confirmed the belief that I just wasn't good enough. I never quite measured up.

Over the years, this belief put a stranglehold on my life to the point where I was dangerously close to an eating disorder. Black market drugs, starving then binging, and exercising to the point of harming my body were my norm.

I didn't even care that I was harming my health in every respect, as long as I could finally be good enough in my body.

As my relationship with God matured, I became painfully aware of the fact that I was not experiencing the freedom promised in the Bible, although I didn't have the understanding of what was really keeping me from experiencing that freedom. I tried diet after diet after diet (including the Christian weight loss programs), thinking that this time, this diet, would surely be the one that would get my body where I wanted it to be. Because of my repeated attempts to lose weight using everything from starving myself to trying to "pray it away," I disrupted my metabolism to the point where even if I did lose weight, I gained it back and wound up weighing more than I did before I started that particular round of dieting. It was a vicious cycle that kept me deeply depressed, lacking self-confidence, and bound by negative self-talk. When I reached a very tight size 16, I knew I couldn't continue going in the same direction, or I was not only going to end up with severe health issues, I was going to jeopardize receiving all God had for my life. Those days were some of the darkest I've known.

Some people may say that food addiction doesn't compare to alcoholism or drug addiction in its intensity. But those of us who have been bound by emotional eating and food addiction know that these traps are just as damaging as any other addiction. I knew if I didn't get control of this part of my life, I was going to lose so much of what God had for me, and in a big way. Part of what made my journey so difficult is that the Church, as a general rule, doesn't address food addiction very often, if ever. Once, when I tried to talk to a pastor about my feelings of bondage, he laughed and said there was no such thing as emotional eating. I felt very lost and alone.

My rock bottom came in the form of a revelation of sorts. I saw myself rock climbing, yet I couldn't go very high because there were so many chains clipped to my rock climbing belt, weighing me down and keeping me from being able to go higher. Slowly but surely, God started showing me what this vision meant as He began speaking to me about what each chain represented. I was bound by emotional eating. Food was my god and my drug of choice. I was bound by self-limiting beliefs around my worth. I was accusing God of not making me good enough. I was choosing to be bound by relationships that hindered rather than supported my spiritual and emotional growth. I was devastated when I realized I had spent years trying to "fix" my outside, when the issues I faced started in my heart. I suddenly realized why all the diets in the world couldn't help me, because what I needed was the inner transformation that would set me free and allow me to have peace in my relationship with food, remove it as the idol I had made it in my life, and in turn, create the kind of health that wholly reflects His glory in spirit, soul, and body.

Thus began my journey to freedom from emotional eating. Divine appointments with incredible health teachers, coaches who understood what letting go of self-limiting beliefs could do for you, and gaining a greater revelation of what it really means to be a "new creature in Christ" have all been part of my journey. Old things were passing away for me, and all things were becoming new. It was during this time I was introduced to the incredible world of raw and living foods. Discovering the gifts God has given us from His garden also came with the realization that embracing a high-raw-food diet was a whole-person lifestyle change. It was exactly what I needed to support me as I renewed my mind to the power of life-giving foods the way God created them. Little did I realize that as I released one chain after another and embraced the power that comes with eating from God's garden, not only would I taste freedom in my relationship with food, I would also begin a transformation in my life's purpose.

My coaching company, Ginny Edwards International, was birthed as a direct result of my journey to freedom from emotional eating. I had a good job, a great job as a matter of fact, in corporate America. I was content. But the more I tasted freedom from emotional eating and the more I created radiant health as a result of eating a high-raw-food diet, I felt a stirring in my heart that I now realize was God calling me to a higher purpose than the one I had currently been living. It became clear to me that the Lord was calling me to create a business that empowered other Christian women to finally and permanently make peace with their bodies, their food, and their health.

Thus began the second part of my journey, which has been a miracle in and of itself. I've watched in awe as God brought the right business and life coaches into my life to give me the knowledge I needed to create a business that empowers women to wholly live their message. I went from being desperate to lose weight, to falling in love with raw food, to the whole-person transformation that comes from changing your diet to one of life-giving foods, to desiring to help other women lose weight, to finally realizing that

I am called to help other women who know they're called to some form of leadership, yet know their health is keeping them from being all they're called to be. It's been a fascinating discovery of how God provides when you take steps of obedience and let go of all the things that hold you back. The most fascinating part of all is realizing that your "rock bottom" is truly a beautiful place to be because it's there you surrender, and it's from that place you can really start living God's rhythm for your life.

Interestingly enough, I recently had a second vision that continued the rock-climbing scenario. I was just about at the summit. But there was a huge protruding boulder I would have to climb up and over to reach my final destination. It was at that moment I saw the whole picture. My Savior, the Lover of my soul, was waiting for me. He reached down, taking my hand, and lifted me over the boulder so I could get to Him. For me, that boulder represented the years of bondage I had experienced as an emotional eater. He was there all the time, reaching out to me, wanting to set me free and take me to His highest and best for my life. That's why I'm so grateful for my rock bottom story.

Ginny Edwards is the CEO and founder of Ginny Edwards International, a coaching company dedicated to empowering women of faith to wholly live their message—spirit, soul, and body. She is one of the leading raw food coaches in the Christian community and has a special passion for coaching women who have been chronic dieters and desire to be free in their relationship with food and with their bodies. Ginny lives in the southern part of the U.S. and continues her training and personal growth by working with some of the world's most successful female entrepreneurs and coaches, and is committed to serving others through the power of her relationship with God through Jesus Christ.

A Loving Father's Embrace

Wherefore he saith, Awake thou that sleepest, and arise from the dead, and Christ shall give thee light. – Ephesians 5:14 (KJV)

Elayna Fernandez-Bare

My eyes felt heavy and were tightly shut, yet I felt as if I were waking from a blurry dream. I could hear my brother's desperate cry, begging, *"Please, take care of her! Don't worry about me—I'm fine!"*

Others were insisting, *"There's not much we can do for her. She won't make it."* I could feel the chaos around me and I gradually became aware of what was occurring. They were talking about *me*.

I was going to die.

The memories of the crash suddenly rushed through my head. We lived far from school, and though we usually took public transportation, some friends had offered to take us home. We felt lucky and safer, ironically...until a thoughtless motorcycle driver got in the way, and my friend lost control of the car.

Upon impact, my heart felt like it had stopped, and darkness enveloped me. From the back seat, I looked through the front windshield directly up at the sky, and in a fraction of a second, I saw the most beautiful constellation of bright stars on the darkest sky I could ever imagine.

I felt like I was falling into a profound abyss.

No one was drinking or speeding or distracted, yet the car did a few full cartwheels, went across the median into the opposite lane, and smashed against a palm tree, ejecting everyone from the car.

Except for me. I was trapped.

Somehow, I was watching all of this happen. Not with my own eyes, but from somewhere above…sort of. Words fail me whenever I try to explain this. My "special" aerial view revealed the driver sitting on the sidewalk, as if in disbelief. My brother had a few scrapes here and there, but he wept, as if his heart were breaking. The guy who occupied the passenger's seat hit his head badly, so I'm guessing he ended up having a couple of stitches.

They were all in fear, shock, and a strange kind of calm panic. I seemed unconscious to them, although my mind seemed more conscious than ever—of people's feelings, their thoughts, of my own emotions, my surroundings, of the past, the present, and the future. I saw other vague images of noisy ambulances and could hear alarmed voices as I was rushed to the hospital.

As I came back to the present moment, I was lying on a hospital bed, unable to move, surprised to find that I felt nothing instead of the unimaginable pain I expected. I realized that night that at only nineteen years of age, I had a very slim chance of survival. I was not expected to make it through the night.

And…I was okay with that. As a matter of fact, I was relieved.

Intrigued, almost fascinated, I began to wonder exactly what was happening. I started paying attention to everything that I could hear and see. Why did some of it seem fuzzy and distant, while other parts could be viewed with unfathomable clarity? I was locked in a coma, had nineteen broken bones, an oxygen mask over my mouth and nose, and a tube coming out of my side.

Soon, the self-pity washed over and through me. I couldn't feel my legs or my tongue or my teeth. For a while, I was very concerned that if I did survive, my teeth would be gone! That feels silly now.

Some of my memories are hazy, but I can recall vividly my dad reacting to the news. I somehow saw him travel for two hours to see me, hoping I would still be alive at his arrival. I saw my mom in pain, sadness rippling across her face. My brother seemed fine, but sad, depressed, and semi-lifeless. My little sisters, my little brother, and my stepmom were confused and feeling helpless.

My soul seemed to be wandering to and fro, and most of the time I saw all white or all black surrounding me. Everyone was so sad and they were losing sleep. It was extremely torturous. Why was it taking so long? It all seemed like a mental prison and I wanted to die already!

The truth is, I felt dead long before the crash. My days had been filled with agony, affliction, and trauma. My nights seemed endless with the same constant nightmare. I could not look in the mirror without feeling disgusted, and I cried myself to sleep wishing the flashbacks would just go away.

I had spent the last six months navigating through hopelessness, self-hate, insecurity, and darkness. I was angry at myself, angry at others, and angry at God. I had kept a positive attitude throughout an emotionally scarring and dysfunctional childhood, through poverty, through hunger, and major hardship…but the pain of reliving that horrible night in March was still unbearable. As I lay weightless, even nearing death, I was still angry.

The events unfolded again in every single, obscene detail. I could see his fierce eyes filled with evil desire like a merciless beast...and I was his prey. I felt his despicable and invasive touch. I listened to the filthy vulgar words he said to me, each and every one of them. How could God have allowed this foul stranger to hold me captive, beat me senseless, and sexually assault me ever so brutally?

In my state, I could not sob or scream, but my spirit was still overcome with fear, rejection, and feelings of unworthiness. This vile monster had threatened to kill me…and how I wished he had!

I was on the verge of dying again, and it hurt me that I had to live with the tormenting shame that filled my heart, with the graphic visuals that filled my mind, with the emptiness that "filled" my spirit.

I could feel the pain of his giant-like hands slapping my face, pulling my hair out in chunks, making me bleed, tearing up my clothing, and using me at his disposal. I had been weak and tried to fight with what little strength I'd had, but then again, what did that accomplish? This thought upset me even more as I impatiently awaited a sweet death that would take it all away.

As I drowned in my rock bottom of self-loathing, I felt my dad's hand touch mine. He was sitting there, and his presence comforted me. That touch gave me a peace and shared a calmness that I had never felt before. I wished I could embrace my daddy and tell him I loved him. I focused all my attention on him as he told me I had to make a choice.

"Don't give up! God spared your life once. It is a miracle you escaped that horror alive. You can decide to live. God gave you a chance, and now it's time to give yourself one!"

His simple, yet powerful, words pierced my core. My Father in Heaven had shown me His infinite love by delivering me from that savage. The car in which he had held me captive for hours simply stopped working. I escaped and he was caught. How did I not see it like a titanic miracle before? I had been so wrapped up in these giant lies about myself for so long, and in a fraction of a second, divine truth began to set me free.

I had thought I was at fate's mercy, and now my earthly father assured me that I had a say. I could fight as hard as I fought earlier that year, and if I would only ask God as fervently as I had asked Him the first time, He would shower me with mercy, love, and healing.

He had never abandoned me. I had abandoned Him. I tasted the sweetness of my Maker's forgiveness as I consciously repented in my very unconsciousness. His forgiveness took away the heavy load of suffering, and all burden, guilt, shame, weakness, failure, sorrow, and despair.

It was a beautiful, sacred moment that I will cherish and remember. Like a prodigal daughter, I was dead, I was lost, and He welcomed me home.

I eventually awoke from my seemingly irreversible coma, but most importantly, I awoke to the infinite love of God, to the love of my family, and to the love of life. I realized that I was never alone, that I am precious to Him. As I write this, my body has been restored, the nightmares are gone, and the images that once overcame me cannot even be triggered as a memory. I see each day as a priceless gift, with blessings in abundance.

It is in the deepest of brokenness where we fully realize that we can be made whole again through His unspeakable light. Even as we are literally or figuratively beaten, rejected, mocked, and tortured, *we are purified, made spotless, and refined.* I am humbled to be a living testimony of His light and for the wondrous opportunity to guide other women toward the joy, balance, and success that only He provides. I honor my earthly father for his unconditional love and wisdom, and praise my Heavenly Father for His tender mercies. I am infinitely grateful for the intense conviction that, through the coldest of trials, I will always be welcome in both my fathers' warm embrace.

Elayna Fernandez-Bare is known worldwide as The Positive MOM. She empowers, equips, and encourages moms of all ages and stages to BE POSITIVE and discover, live, balance, monetize, and radiate their passions so they can create joy, balance, and success on their own terms without mommy guilt, stress, burnout, inertia, or overwhelm. Her philosophy is, "BE Positive and You'll BE Powerful!"

www.ThePositiveMOM.com

ROCK BOTTOM IS A BEAUTIFUL PLACE

Faith In Action

"For I know the plans I have for you," says the LORD. "They are plans for good and not for disaster, to give you a future and a hope. In those days when you pray, I will listen. If you look for me wholeheartedly, you will find me. I will be found by you," says the LORD. "I will end your captivity and restore your fortunes. I will gather you out of the nations where I sent you and will bring you home again to your own land." – Jeremiah 29:11-13 (NLT)

 *Robin Hardy*

I think there are so many times in our lives that we feel like we have hit rock bottom, and I have hit it many times in my journey as a Christian. I was single until the age of thirty-six, lost both parents by this age, went through physical and verbal abuse by guys I dated, and changed everything in my life when I got married to my amazing husband. These changes included leaving my own place, giving up my car, changing my job, and changing my church.

However, the hardest part was the change or the realization that people who I thought were friends were not really so at all. I had unknowingly surrounded myself with people who only came around when they wanted something or they were in crisis. Most of them sat back and watched as I dealt with the many challenges in my own life, when I could have used some form of encouragement. I found that most of those I called friends were only there if I would go to them. It was like pulling teeth to get them to come my direction to hang out.

I have to say the biggest change and biggest rock bottom experience that I've encountered was in our business. I'm not sure why this challenge rocked my world so profoundly, especially when I had previously come through being diagnosed with cancer and knowing that I would never have children because of it. Yet, that rock bottom seemed much easier to cope with than the one we encountered after only six years of marriage. You see, the cancer got healed through faith and prayer, and God brought me a husband who didn't care if we had children or not.

About seven years ago, we had built an amazing business—we were living the life. My husband was able to retire from his job and we worked the business together. The business had multiple lines of revenue, which is what we were taught to do to make sure the cash continued flowing. Yet, we had no idea what would happen when the economy took a dive. We were thankful that we had been good stewards with the money and we had some reserves put away. We saw the wall coming about six months prior to impact.

We hit that wall at full speed, even though we tried to do everything we could to turn it around. We lost everything. We had two homes: one was a rental or investment property, and the other was our primary residence. We had gone to the banks prior to hitting the wall to let them know what was coming our way. We asked them how we could structure this impact so that we could do what was right and ethical. They were of no help to us. They told us that my husband needed to be dead, dying, or I had to divorce him.

We then lost all of our vehicles, which in most cases is not a big deal, except we had no revenue coming in. We were forced into bankruptcy, both corporate and personal, which was one of the hardest things emotionally that hit us. You see, we were raised to believe that if you incurred a debt, you paid it. I was raised with the mindset that bankruptcy meant you had failed. In my mind, all I could see was failure written all over my life.

I took this very personally, and on many occasions, I spent days in the living room, crying out to God, "Where are you?" Numerous occasions had my mother-in-law reinforcing what a failure I was. She would ask, how could I do this to her son? She also told me constantly that God was punishing us for something. The funny thing was, when Greg or I would ask her what it was she thought we were getting punished for, she would turn away and ignore us. We soon came to realize that when other people are dealing with issues in their lives, they shake their finger at you because it makes them feel better.

So why has this been my greatest rock bottom story? The number one reason that most marriages end is due to finances. Because both Greg and I profess our faith openly, because we love Jesus Christ, and because we try to live our lives according to His will, we became a marked target for people who wanted to know when we failed.

What I learned through this rock bottom experience is that:

- Faith and trust in God is essential
- We are not defined by our circumstances
- We are constantly being observed by other believers and nonbelievers alike
- Our choice to act versus react changed many lives and saved many marriages
- We always have a choice to get up, dust ourselves off, and move forward, or sit around and have a pity party

Since that period in our life, we have been able to start fresh, reinvent ourselves, and keep moving forward. It has also reinforced that nothing is impossible with God in our life, and through Him we can do anything. Through this journey, I learned how good the enemy is, attacking the mind as you try to hold tight to your faith. Plus we still, to this day, encounter issues because of the circumstances so many years ago. However, the fact that we follow Jesus Christ and we have a hope eternal gets us through each and every challenge that is added to this particular rock bottom.

By sharing this journey with you, the fear that I have is your judgment for the choices I made, the fear of being labeled as the world will label me (and even as I labeled myself). Through the sharing, my hope is that anyone reading this will also understand that their circumstances do not determine who they are. Who we are is determined by our actions as we come through the circumstances we encounter in life.

I know that rock bottom is a beautiful place because it allows us to take the time to examine who we are and how we respond to the events and trials in our lives. Rock bottom is also a place where we can draw closer to God, develop our character, and build our faith in Him. Rock bottom allowed me to go back to the basics, to go back to the essentials in life, and to be a resource for anyone else on that journey.

You see, rock bottom is not a place of failure. Rock bottom is a place that God allows us to build our character so that we can empower other people and encourage them during their trials and circumstances. This rock bottom experience is a very powerful one that drew my husband and I closer together, reinforced our faith in Christ, and allowed us to be a witness and example to other marriages that were encountering the same circumstances. This was a beautiful place because it allowed our faith to grow, our relationship to grow, and from what I heard after the fact, our example of how we handled the circumstances actually saved other marriages. So in that light, rock bottom is a beautiful place. The key to it, however, is we don't stay there. We get up, brush off our knees, and keep moving forward.

Let's just say that rock bottom, in most cases, is what you call "faith in action."

Robin Hardy took the leap of faith to start her own business after fourteen years in corporate America, and has been a business owner for over eleven years. Robin focuses on empowering women entrepreneurs to take the next step in their businesses by supporting them virtually, and identifying and implementing systems and programs to take their businesses to the next level. Robin lives with her husband Greg and four furry babies: Charley Brown, Lucie Ball, Ashley and her new baby, Zeus the Moose. You can learn more about Robin's business services at http:// integrityvaservices.com.

A Mother's Journey Through Grief

It is, I think, that we are all so alone in what lies deepest in our souls, so unable to find the words, and perhaps the courage to speak with unlocked hearts, that we don't know at all that it is the same with others.
– Sheldon Vanauken

Eileen Holtry

On a Friday morning around 11:00 a.m., I received a phone call that would change my life forever.

Earlier that day, when I awakened my children for school, no one wanted to go except for Chris. It was the Friday before spring break and half of the kids at school would be starting their vacations early. However, Chris wanted to attend a party that had been planned for his men's choir group. The teacher had ordered breakfast burritos. For a fourteen-year-old boy, a class party that included free breakfast burritos was just too good to pass up. It was a warm, beautiful, sunny March day when I dropped him at school that morning, and I will never forget the smile on his face as he waved goodbye and told me he loved me.

When our receptionist interrupted my meeting later that morning to let me know I had an urgent call holding, I could tell by the tone of her voice that something was tragically wrong. It was my daughter on the other end of the line. "It's Chris. There has been an accident. You need to get there as soon as possible."

My heart began to beat rapidly and my mind raced. Why was he not at school? What could have happened? Why was my daughter so distraught? As I prepared to leave, one of my co-workers insisted that she drive. One glance at the look on everyone's faces as I walked out of the building that day told me everything I needed to know. My son was gone.

The first thing I saw as we pulled into the driveway was the sheriff's vehicles, and my stomach began to churn. I stepped out of the car and my son's friend, Kris, approached me. Our eyes met and I saw the tears streaming down his face. My head now had to accept what I already knew in my heart. My legs could not support my weight, and I collapsed into a heap on the ground, sobbing uncontrollably, my heart breaking inside of me.

My son had left school shortly after I had dropped him off. Maybe this was a spontaneous decision or something that had been planned earlier. I'll never know. Kris's mom had gone out of town, and he had found the keys to her car that was parked in the garage. He had come by school and picked up my son, along with some other friends, and they spent the next couple of hours cruising around town.

They were being kids and enjoying the moment.

After arriving back at Kris's home, they took turns driving the small, modified sports vehicle around the quiet, gated neighborhood. With little driving experience, my son got behind the wheel of the car while another boy rode shotgun.

"They were having a grand time," a neighbor related to me years later. She had seen them from her kitchen window doing loops around the small community, smiling and laughing as they drove by. Then, she saw the accident. My son lost control of the car as he skidded in some gravel and went through a guardrail into the culvert below. He died on impact. The boy riding shotgun walked away. At almost eight months pregnant, the neighbor, Kathy, ran out of the house, down the hill, and waded into the shallow water. She pulled my son from the vehicle and proceeded to perform CPR. She attempted to save him, but it was too late.

The days, weeks, and months following the accident were a blur. Each morning required a huge effort to get out of bed, placing one foot in front of the other, and would be done only because my two surviving children were depending on me. My children were devastated and so was I. How could God have allowed this to happen? Had I not already been through enough pain? I had been through an abusive marriage, then a bitter and costly divorce, and now this. How was I going to survive this catastrophic loss? I could hear Job's wife in my head…or was it Satan whispering in my ear? *Curse God and die.* I could have easily done just that. They say a person can die of a broken heart, and mine felt like it was being crushed in a vice. To die would have been a relief.

This was my rock bottom. Everything I believed about myself and my faith was tested. Everything I believed about my God was questioned. How could I ever trust God again? What was I supposed to believe any more when I prayed? Why would I pray at all when a sovereign God who held all of my hopes and dreams in His hands would fail me this way? I questioned God's wisdom and His judgment. I doubted His love and His faithfulness, but one thing I never doubted or denied was that He was God and still in control. But the wall that had been erected around my heart from past hurts and disappointments was now a fortress.

I put on a mask and tried to survive the best I could, but behind that mask was a depressed and angry person, unable to laugh or experience joy. I resented others whose sons were growing up and becoming young men, graduating from high school, going off to college, getting married. All of the milestones that are a parent's joy were being denied me. And my anger, as much as I tried to hide it, seeped out of my locked heart and hurt those closest to me.

While I struggled with my faith and how to endure the loss of my son, God's love and grace sustained me as He patiently walked me through my grief, asking me to trust Him. Though it took many more years for the wound to heal and the rawness of my pain to subside, I quit questioning and asking, "Why?" I accepted that God in His sovereignty had allowed this tragedy for His own reasons, which I will never know this side of heaven. What I do know is that my son is gone from my presence, and yet, because of Jesus, he lives and one day I will see him again. For now, I have his memories, which I hold close to my heart until I can once again hold him in my arms. In the meantime, God continues to hold me in His and show me His comfort. Through His love and patience, my heart has been softened and my faith strengthened. And I am now able to share my story and comfort others.

As I sat having lunch with Kathy years after the accident, she poured out her heart and her tears as she apologized for not doing something more that day to prevent my son's death. I was able to forgive her and reassure her that it was not her fault. No one was to blame. I never saw her again, but had extended grace to her that day, grace that she so desperately needed and the freedom from guilt that she had carried for so many years.

I don't know what kind of loss you might be experiencing in your life—maybe it is the loss of a job, or a marriage, or a child. Maybe you are carrying guilt or anger that has locked your heart and kept you from experiencing the joy and freedom Jesus died to give you. Please know that you are not alone. Reach out and connect with others along this journey. For it is in community that we experience Christ's compassion, healing, and restoration. Today, I encourage you to surrender your wounded heart to God and allow Him to take your pain and grief and give you His everlasting comfort.

Eileen Holtry left a career in the corporate world to pursue her God-given dreams and is an aspiring author, speaker, and life coach, and the owner of Eileen Holtry Fine Art, an online Christian art gallery. She is passionate about growing in God's revealed truth and becoming all that He created her to be, inspiring others to do the same. She loves traveling, reading, hiking, and spending time with family, especially her children and granddaughter. Visit www.eileenholtryfineart.com to learn more about Eileen.

Dancing In The Fire

Behold, I have refined thee, but not with silver; I have chosen thee in the furnace of affliction. – Isaiah 48:10 (KJV)

And I will bring the third part through the fire, and refine them as silver is refined, and try them as gold is tried: they shall call on my name, and I will hear them: I will say, It [is] my people: and they shall say the Lord is my God. – Zechariah 13:9 (KJV)

Benita Ibrahim

When I was younger, we had a house fire. It was said to have started in the walls, and it was ruled an electrical fire. Everything was lost in a blink of an eye that day, including a family member and one who was severely burned. My parents were devastated with grief, financial worry, and the nagging questions: "What will we do?" "Where will we live?" "Where will we go?" It's been over twenty-five years now, and God has been faithful and purposeful in everything concerning us. All that we lost in the fire, God restored tenfold! Only He can turn a destitute situation with no hope into beauty for ashes. He uses those unfortunate circumstances of hopelessness to make us stronger, to draw us closer to Him, and to transform us to be used for His glory!

When we think of fire, we naturally think of it as being a very bad thing. After all, fire is very destructive—it's harmful, it kills, it steals from you, and it can destroy everything in its path. Because of my experience growing up, fire has always been a very negative (but powerful) element to me. I saw it quickly devastate and change lives around me. It robbed us of memories, things, and people we can never get back. If you have ever been burned, you never forget the experience from that one incident. The memory of it can be very traumatic and painful. Some burns go away without scarring, while others may remain, leaving a nasty scar that transforms that area forever…

In elementary school I loved art class because this was the only place I could create something beautiful out of whatever the teacher gave us. She also gave us the freedom to control how elaborate we wanted our project to be, or we could just choose to do nothing at all with it. One day we were given a project with the instructions of taking a ball of clay and creating serving dishes out of it by using the imprint of our hand (I know we ALL remember this!). The teacher gave us the tools we needed to complete the project and wrote down the process so we wouldn't forget. I remember the excitement and anticipation I felt molding the clay and creating this wonderful work of art. I watched the teacher go to each student and glance at their work with a smile that said, "Good job!" She walked over and heated the oven to place our clay dishes in and patiently waited. As we continued molding the clay, I remember the uncertainty of knowing exactly how much pressure to place onto the clay to make the perfect carbon copy of my hand. I looked around the room and did a quick observation of everyone's project, hoping it would give me an idea of how much pressure to put on mine.

As they were placed in the oven, the heat began to cause the clay to harden, to take shape and transform the clay into serving dishes. When they were removed from the heat, we noticed that even though we all were given the same clay, the same amount, and the same instructions, we all got different results. There were some that didn't take shape because there wasn't enough pressure placed on them, and the imprint didn't remain in the heat. Others cracked because they had a very thin foundation. Some were unrecognizable because they didn't follow instructions. Then, there were dishes that were given just the right amount of pressure and heat to transform the ball of clay into a beautiful replica of the maker's handprint, creating a beautiful masterpiece.

This is how our heavenly Father is with us. Through life's journeys of heartaches and brokenness (the fire), He uses those situations to mold us and shape us into His image. The refiner's fire sets us apart and brings us to holiness. Because He loves us so much, He allows us to experience brokenness to create beautiful masterpieces as we walk through the "fires" of life.

I have come to understand that all "fire" isn't bad and used for destruction. Some of the greatest and strongest things in life are made from the hottest fires. It's only through the refiner's "fire" (whether it be divorce, separation, death, a prodigal child, an unbelieving spouse, sickness, cancer, blended family issues, addiction, financial issues, homelessness, abandonment, foster care, rejection, hopelessness, loneliness, despair and depression, etc.) that we are purified, purged, and cleansed. The definition for transformation is "a complete change or act of changing." I thought this was significant because "fire" is also used to change something from one state to another.

Not long ago, my precious mother passed from breast cancer. She resided with us for over fifteen years and was a wonderful example of God's redemption, grace, and faith. The cancer was very aggressive and metastasized quickly throughout her body, and she had to have a mastectomy and became paralyzed. It was so difficult to see the loss of hair, strength, and life from someone once so strong and vivacious as she was reduced to skin and bones. However, she may have lost her life here on earth, but she never lost her light! She never complained, and she refused to take anything for pain. She would just say, "This too shall pass."

During this time, we experienced financial hardships, and I had to drop out of working toward my master's. I started experiencing chronic vertigo and migraines, I couldn't stand up or lay down, and I was taking nine pills a day. One afternoon I felt a burning sensation in my head, not realizing the left side of my face was paralyzed. I was diagnosed with Bell's palsy due to stress. God was bringing everything to the surface in order to make me whole!

The stress, days without sleep, and mother's constant throwing up and diarrhea due to chemo and radiation began to break me. We had to make some hard decisions regarding one of our children and prayed not to get that dreaded call no parent wants to ever hear. The strain of everything put stress on my marriage and depression slowly began to set in. This was a very painful season in my life, and this is when I hit Rock Bottom. In my brokenness, I leaned on God like never before for strength and comfort. Reading one day, I began to weep before the Lord. I turned to Isaiah 61 and I was encouraged *"[H]e has sent me to bind up the brokenhearted…and provide for those that grieve in Zion—to bestow on them a crown of beauty instead of ashes, the oil of joy instead of mourning, and a garment of praise instead of a spirit of despair. They will be called oaks of righteousness, a planting of the Lord for the display of his splendor"* (v. 1,3 NIV). It was then I had clarity—my brokenness wasn't just for me, but for others.

When the hurt became so loud that I couldn't hear His voice, I put my hope and trust in His word and learned to dance in the fire. I now understand that He had a purpose and plan for everything we were going through, even when we couldn't see it.

When we come to the end of ourselves through brokenness, we find healing, restoration, and transformation. We come to know God is our hope, and He will never leave us nor forsake us in the midst of the "fire." God can use a man greatly when he's wounded deeply. His desire is to take us from brokenness to beauty so we may encourage someone else to dance through the fire as well.

Those that sow in tears will reap with songs of joy. He who goes out weeping, carrying seeds to sow, will return with songs of joy, carrying sheaves with him (Ps. 126:5-6).

Benita Ibrahim has been a small business owner for over twenty years. She is the founder and director of a daycare facility in Texas. Her life's passion is to empower women through her philanthropy work and to bring encouragement, healing, and comfort to women on their life's journey. Her heart's desire is to use the talents and gifts God has given her as a platform to glorify Him and uplift women all over the world. She strongly believes your pain is your ministry, and your mess is your message. Benita resides in Texas with her husband, and they have two amazing sons, three beautiful daughters, six grandchildren and two godchildren. www.beautifulcolorsdaycare.com.

Putting On a New Self

You were taught, with regard to your former way of life, to put off your old self, which is being corrupted by its deceitful desires; to be made new in the attitude of your minds; and to put on the new self, created to be like God in true righteousness and holiness. – Ephesians 4:22-24 (NIV)

Heidi Kleine

Even though I can remember the exact moment I realized I was at rock bottom, hindsight has shown me there were several moments I had missed that led up to it.

The summer of 2010 was an exciting time in my life. As a stay-at-home mom, my life revolved around my daughters. My oldest daughter was graduating from high school and had been accepted into her first-choice college. That same weekend, my second daughter was getting confirmed, a major milestone in our family of faith. With so much pride for these beautiful young women, we were planning a huge party, inviting all our family and friends to join us. I had much to celebrate.

Even though my head told me I should be proud of myself for raising these girls, I could not get my heart wrapped around that thought. For months leading up to this moment, I had planned on losing some weight, but life always got in the way. As family and friends gathered that weekend, I was at my highest weight ever—nearly 300 pounds. I found a great dress and got caught up in the celebration, forgetting how I had hoped to be healthier. Afterwards, there were so many wonderful pictures from the event. There I stood, clearly proud and happy for my girls, but so obviously tired and sick in my own body. I was horrified by this image of myself.

I remember hearing a devotion on the radio shortly after seeing those pictures. The speaker was referring to Christ's message to us that we are to love one another as we love ourselves. Loving ourselves was the first step. He challenged me to write in my Bible, "I love me so that I can love God." When I followed his instructions, I had tears in my eyes, because I knew I really didn't believe those words. However, I wasn't quite at rock bottom yet.

Rock bottom came a little over a month later. During this time, my dear friend was in the midst of her battle with terminal brain cancer. She had been diagnosed the fall before and we were blessed that treatments were allowing for some quality time together that summer.

Gigi and I had been friends for many years. She was the first person that I met when my family located to North Carolina. We were both extroverts married to introverts, daughters of Lutheran pastors, mothers of daughters, Girl Scout leaders, and the list goes on and on. We had spent many hours planning our future, and we were on a mission to pass our faith on to future generations. We were going to be awesome mother-in-laws and grandmothers.

By the time of my rock bottom moment, we both understood that none of our plans were going to come to fruition. One particularly difficult afternoon as we sat together, I said I wished there was something I could do to make everything better. I expected that she would commiserate with me about our lost dreams. Instead, she said, "It would give me peace to know that you had found a better way to handle your stress than to take it out on your body."

That really struck a nerve. She was asking me to deal with the most challenging issue of my life. I know she understood losing her was going to be one of the hardest things I had ever faced. She did not want her death to put me in an even unhealthier state. She knew that food was my go-to solution for stress and loneliness, and that losing her was going to bring stress and loneliness to my life in a major way.

Although I knew her words came from a place of love, I was so sad when I left that day. How could I ever possibly grant her this peace? I had never succeeded at facing this challenge in the past, but to honor our friendship, I had no choice but to face this challenge now.

As I pondered her statement, I reflected back on everything she was going through as she fought for her life. I felt a shift in my perspective. If the tables were turned and there had been things that she chose not to do to survive, I would have been so angry with her. Suddenly I saw my choices in a different light. I came face-to-face with the reality that my actions were choices. Every day, I was making choices that jeopardized my long-term health, and I was justifying my weight by blaming everything but my choices.

Sure, my life was challenging. Raising four daughters, dealing with financial stress, and navigating marriage were all challenges, but not excuses for my choices. I had become so comfortable taking care of everyone else that somewhere along the course of my life, I lost sight of my own value. I had come to see myself as the least important thing on the agenda. Since I did not see my own value, I spent my time proving my worth to the world. It wasn't enough to just be a mom; I had to be super mom. It wasn't enough to volunteer to help at the school carnival; I had to be the chair. I used my weight as proof that I was not good enough and focused on everything else to try and address the perception that I wasn't enough. Gigi's statement helped me realize that the only way out was going to be prioritizing myself and making the right choices for me before all else.

Once I realized that this was going to come down to me choosing to be healthy, opportunities appeared in my path. I became open to the idea that there might be a solution. Although I knew the basics of what I needed to do, I knew enough about myself and my history to know that I needed help. For the first time, I asked for it. What I did not do was ask for anyone's permission to take the time or money to take care of myself.

I started a food plan and joined a wonderful fitness program, things that I had previously thought would take too much time and money away from my family. I found the people that could help me, and I respected their knowledge and authority. I followed their directions. As I began to lose the weight, I learned the amazing value of feeling strong. As I conquered physical challenges at the gym, I found myself standing up for myself at home and at work. A colleague commented that my voice grew in direct proportion to how my body shrank. In the process, I also began to peel away the layers of shame and guilt. I learned that I was abusing food. I ate when I was lonely or felt like the events of my life were out of my control. I needed to admit that this was an unhealthy addiction and treat it accordingly.

The most amazing part of this journey for me was how it strengthened my faith. As I struggled with all of these moments of clarity and challenge, I found myself looking to God's Word in a new way. I felt convicted by the reality He provided me all I needed to be strong and healthy—whole, nutritious, bountiful food and the opportunity to use my body to its full potential. I came to understand I had fallen victim to the seduction of the marketing and greed in the food and weight loss industry. The more I have learned about how food has been manipulated, the more convinced I have become I am called to share my story. I am called to educate and share my knowledge and experience with women who face a similar struggle.

Every time I read the verse from Ephesians, I visualize myself taking off the extra one hundred pound self with all her baggage and setting her aside. I have lived without her for several years now. My new self thrives in the strength of her body, the strength of her mind, and the strength of her faith.

Gigi passed away in January, six months after our conversation. At that time, I had lost thirty of the one hundred pounds that I would eventually lose. She knew my mindset had changed. She knew I had found a better way to deal with my stress. I believe she got her peace. On the day of her funeral, I sent my trainer a text that read: "Just between you and me, and because I know Gigi would love to hear it, I'm feeling pretty awesome in my little black dress."

Heidi Kleine is an inspirational speaker, author, coach, and Christian Faith Formation professional. Her motto for life is "Strong Body, Strong Mind, Strong Faith." Mother to four beautiful daughters, Heidi spent years living in a state of overwhelm, overweight, and over-commitment, all while being undernourished physically and spiritually. A one hundred pound weight loss and life transformation led Heidi to start her own coaching practice in order to share her insights with other women who find themselves in similar circumstances. You can find more information at www.heidikleinecoaching.com.

From 35,000 Feet to Rock Bottom to Grace

The greatest chapters in history always begin with risk, and the same is true with the chapters of your life. If you don't take the risk, you forfeit the miracle.
– Mark Batterson

Kathi Laughman

My rock bottom realization happened onboard a Boeing 757. About to travel at an altitude of 35,000 feet, I found myself at rock bottom. I didn't realize what a tailspin I had been in until I got on that plane.

The seatbelt would not reach across my lap. Progressive weight gain over the years brought me to that moment where I had to ask the flight attendant for an extension. Mortified? Yes. Disgusted? Yes. Discouraged? Undeniably, yes. Everything I had tried had failed: diets, programs, and even a personal trainer. While my body simply would not melt, my spirit could—and it had.

Over time it seemed that everywhere in my life, I bumped against a growing emptiness. My daughter had gotten married. Undoubtedly, this was a happy "moving on" for everyone, including me. However, there was also a marked sadness. I had been a single parent for most of her life, which meant the emptying of the nest was more pronounced. Within a year, my new son-in-law's job presented them with a great opportunity, but it meant they had to move to another state. It was great news for them, but very sad for me. My emptiness grew deeper.

I did as many of us do when one part of our life transitions: I poured myself into my work. Having a successful career already, I was now completely free to dedicate myself to that work. No glass ceilings for me; I soared! But that emptiness was still there.

Then, the day came when other people again made decisions that would impact my life. My executive career came to an abrupt halt when the company I had been an integral part of building was bought out. I found myself without work in very tough economic times. I had now gone from empty nest to empty work. The road ahead was daunting, yet I was determined not to let those buffeting winds of change knock me off my feet.

The day I got on that plane, I was working out what was next for me professionally. Little did I know, I was about to reach a personal breaking point. It may seem insignificant, but when that seat belt would not reach, I felt like everything about my life was spinning out of control. I was done waiting to find out what the next blow might be. I needed to take back control somewhere in my life.

I was determined that this time, I would not fail in my quest to reach a healthy weight. I was tired of losing everything except the fat. I scheduled a doctor's appointment to talk about my options. Many tests later, as I sat in that little room, dressed in yet another clinical garment clearly not designed for someone my size, I had no idea what was in store. A surgical option? A clinical diet? Whatever it was, I knew I was prepared to do it. Another surprise was in store. I wasn't prepared for what the doctor had to say when she joined me. I was actually quite ill, now completing the chain of blows.

Empty nest, empty job, empty health. Emptiness.

"What do you know about hepatitis C?" she asked. At that moment, my world stood still and then began to truly tip into a freefall.

The journey I was about to embark on would take me into valleys I did not even know were there. The diagnosis was clear: I had carried this virus for many years. Unknown to me, my liver was progressively failing. Like millions of my generation, I learned that, while I never felt obviously "sick" from the virus, its toll on my health was unmistakable. Even the weight gain was part of its hold on my well-being.

My next step was to look at my options and find the right doctor to partner with for treatment. God's hand was evident and "Team Kathi" began to assemble. At the medical helm was a remarkable liver specialist, my perfect counterbalance in a fearful situation. His staff became friends over the coming months, without question, angels on earth. A pharmaceutical group came into our band of warriors, and with them came medications and more friends. They all worked diligently on my behalf to both help eradicate the virus and champion cost-effective treatment options. God was bringing people into my life to serve His purpose, and everything fell into place.

From rock bottom, I could and would find my way back up. In her own writings after facing and beating breast cancer, Deena Metzger wrote, "A sacred illness is one that educates us and alters us from the inside out, provides experiences and therefore knowledge that we could not possibly achieve in any other way, and aligns us with a life path that is, ultimately, of benefit to ourselves and those around us." That sentiment became part of my truth.

The journey was not easy. As my body went to war against itself, there were difficult days and endless nights suffering from the side effects of three medications and chemotherapy. There were times I could only stand in the shower and weep to find relief. Physically, it was the most difficult time of my life. The long list of possible side effects just became a checklist of everything I would encounter.

Nine very long months later, I was virus-free. I had every reason to rejoice, but I was simply too devastated physically, mentally, and emotionally from the treatment to go to the party. The win still felt like a loss. During those months, I learned how it felt to want to just give up. Any vestige of vanity I had left was long gone. Above all of the physical debilitation from the drug therapies, the dance with clinical depression was also challenging. However, there was something that served to bring me through—or, rather, someone.

During that time, I had no energy or desire to spend any time in public other than going to labs and doctors' offices, but human interaction was still important. I found myself signing up for online classes. In one of them, the speaker made a casual remark about *The Circle Maker*, a book she was reading by Mark Batterson. It had absolutely nothing to do with her subject matter (social media), but everything to do with what God wanted me to hear. Two days later, my faithful UPS driver handed me the book that would help lead me up from the dark pit I was in and back into God's glory and light.

I put Mark's teachings about our most authentic relationship with God into practice in my daily life. Although a Christian since I was a young girl, these new insights showed me that I had only been scratching the surface. I started my own prayer circle and began to claim God's promises for what was ahead for my life.

Today, I am fully healed and recovered from hepatitis C, but more than my body has been healed. My total being is now on a path to wellness. I am living a life rich with expanded circles beyond that "empty nest." My body of work continues to grow in ways I never could have dreamed possible. My physical health continues to improve daily. There is nothing empty anywhere unless I empty it to make room for more.

As I move beyond this learning chapter of my life, my journey is remarkably different. My vision is clear, my mind is engaged, and my heart is open. As each part of me heals, it allows me to put that time behind me. My hairdresser and I recently laughed about finally cutting off the last of my "chemo" hair. The scars on my skin from other side effects now look like badges of courage. My energy grows with every step I take in my quest to achieve optimal health. My weight goal remains ahead of me, but now it is a matter of making good choices and taking the right steps to get there. Defeat is not part of this new journey.

More importantly, the lessons learned remain in front of me. They are a torch to light the path ahead. I have learned that gratitude and grace cannot be separated; gratitude comes first, not last. I am thankful for every step of my journey, and I anticipate what lies ahead, knowing that, within seemingly dark places, we can discover the most brilliant of lights and claim them as our own.

Kathi Laughman is a best-selling author, inspirational speaker, and certified life strategist. She is the founder and CEO of The Mackenzie Circle LLC, a life coaching and personal leadership company where she champions entrepreneurs as their possibility partner, coach, and mentor. Her personal mission is to inspire, facilitate, and invest in the success of others. Learn more at www.MackenzieCircle.com.

More Than Afraid

Oh, brethren, be great believers! Little faith will bring your souls to heaven, but great faith will bring heaven to your souls. – Charles H. Spurgeon

Jamie LeNoir

I was born into a family of sinners, with some of those sins encompassing incest, adultery, physical abuse, verbal abuse, and the list goes on. I was also born into a family of believers in Jesus Christ: preacher, teacher, deacon, prayer warriors, and other forms of service. I continued this trend of being a sinful believer.

As both a victim and participator in sin, I often recognized the link between choices and consequences. Sex outside of marriage resulted in pregnancy, damaged my witness, and made teaching abstinence to my children a challenge. My father's choice to abuse alcohol and be unfaithful in marriage resulted in my parents' divorce.

But when my terrifying Rock Bottom season came out of nowhere, I was devastated. I couldn't make the connection to choices and consequences. Why was this happening? What had brought this into my life? I cried out, "Jesus! No! No! No! Haven't I had enough?"

> *And his disciples asked him, "Rabbi, who sinned, this man or his parents, that he was born blind?" Jesus answered, "It was not that this man sinned, or his parents, but that the works of God might be displayed in him (John 9: 2-3 ESV).*

Terror became my constant companion—not fear, terror. Deep within my soul was a pain almost too deep to bear. Having been plagued by panic attacks once before, I thought my mental illness was under control. Now, I was unable to drive the freeway, shop for groceries, or sit in a movie theater. Taking a shower was frightening, as I thought the decorative pictures on the bathroom wall were going to attack me. I barely made it through giving a lecture to my students without taking multiple breaks. Driving to and from work felt as though I was traveling cross-country. I spent as much time as I could with my dear friend because I was afraid of myself. I could not trust my own mind. I was sure at any moment I would "snap" and be lost in a world where no one would ever find me. Never had I felt so bleak, so alone, or so very afraid.

My terror continued as I began seeking help and healing. Mental illness is not an easy or inexpensive fix. I had a wonderful Christian counselor, and my weekly sessions increased to three times a week. I began seeing a psychiatrist for medication. Finding the right meds in the correct dosages was horrific. Every medication had some kind of side effect. I experienced worsened anxiety, nightmares, facial tingling, and stomach upset. The worst side effects were the ones that left me feeling suicidal. During this time, my friend and my mom spent the night with me until my new medication would kick in and take effect. At times I truly wanted to be put away, end my life, or be constantly and deeply medicated.

I was personally acquainted with Hell. It was my daily life.

Fears

My greatest fear was the unknown. I could not help but think about whether there would be a medication to help me. Not only did I wonder if I would be helped, but I wondered if I would be healed? I wondered if my future would be harmed by limited brain function or diminished emotional strength. Most of all, how would others respond to me if they really knew the depth of my loss and pain? I feared my internal discomfort would create discomfort for those around me and that they'd avoid me. After all, people are uncomfortable with pain. I did not want pity, apathy, or judgment. Even within the church body, there are those who say "pray more," "it's a faith issue," "stay strong," and many other biblical, but superficial clichés. However, many Rock Bottom experiences require time to walk through each level of grief: denial, anger, bargaining, sadness, and acceptance. Therefore, applying a scriptural "bandage" does not heal when the Lord allows life to hit you head on.

My present fear in sharing this story is a concern that I may be mocked or ridiculed by those who'd want to hurt me. I wonder if I will lose credibility or respect from believers in Christ who may feel my lack of faith or sinful choices were the cause of my season of terror. My greatest fear, however, is for you to think that we have nothing in common. You should not think your stories, your pain, or your need is so different that you lose the comfort of knowing you are not alone. I do not want you to think that, although your choices may have brought you to your present suffering, you are unworthy of His help and love. Please do not be afraid to let Him do His work in you.

Lessons Learned and My Journey Since . . .

We need to allow Him to do a complete cleaning of our wounds. We need help from experts, we need time, love, grace, and truth. We need to let go, be vulnerable, risk rejection, and know some things may be worse before they are better. The journey to healing is so very painful, but absolutely necessary to have a victorious life. Please do not misunderstand a victorious life as a trial-free life. While I am healed from terror and suicidal thoughts, I am not completely healed from mental illness. I live a joyful and loving life with my reality. I will most likely need medication for the rest of my life. I have seasons of seeing my therapist when my anxiety climbs. I see a psychiatrist to monitor medication benefits and side effects. I have to be very careful not to isolate and withdraw from people. I need structure, exercise, friends, and time outdoors. I've learned that I am very needy. My need keeps me humble, seeking the Lord, and helps me not to judge others for the decisions they make that are guided by their own unhealed wounds.

Rock Bottom Beauty

I know that Rock Bottom is a beautiful place because the depth of my pain caused me to embrace the Lord during a time and place of great suffering. I know Him now in a way I never have before; He truly is deeper and greater than my pain. I no longer have simple head knowledge of what scripture teaches about Jesus; I have the richest, most beautifully intimate and unimagined connection with the Most High God. Not only do I better appreciate the suffering of Jesus, I appreciate the role of suffering in the life of others.

Sadly, for most of us, we only seek the Lord's comfort and connection when we feel uncomfortable and disconnected from a life of ease. I now work hard to avoid saving others from their pain with my simple tips or quick fixes, and instead allow the Lord to set the pace for their healing. Rock Bottom has also taught me that healing may not come in the way I think it should. Healing may be my acceptance of change, loss, or suffering instead of going back to the ways things were before tragedy struck. I seek less to figure things out and instead seek to know Him more.

Jamie LeNoir has been teaching communication studies at the college level for fifteen years, loving and encouraging her students toward healthy communication skills. Recently, she developed Active4Him to more specifically teach women the value of being active in faith and fitness for Christ. Jamie lives with her wonderful husband, three dogs, three cats and treasures her newest role as Nana. www.Active4Him.com

Learning to Breathe Again

And the peace of God, which surpasses all understanding, will guard your hearts and your minds in Christ Jesus. – Philippians 4:7 (ESV)

Karen Lindwall-Bourg

Perhaps many rock bottom experiences begin with a mountaintop experience; however, not every rock bottom experience ends on the mountaintop. Our trip to rock bottom began with the release of a grain of sand. Soon we were trying to keep our balance while slipping and sliding downward over pebbles and skinning our knees on stumbling stones. Boulders came crashing down around us as we slid into the suffocating swamplands of rock bottom, each breath becoming more labored and difficult. Maybe it takes living and breathing through the crisp, thin air of the mountaintop, then coming down, to understand and survive the heavy air in the lowest chasm of rock bottom.

I was a college student working through the divorce of my parents and the loss of my first real love when my mother introduced me to Tim. He was a deacon in her church, and assigned to care for and oversee Mom and my sister. I knew immediately that Tim was the one for me. I was attracted to his love for the Lord, his maturity in leadership, his infectious smile, and blue eyes. We married in a wonderful ceremony surrounded not just by biological family, but also by Tim's extended Guatemala missionary family. We began to build a life together and soon were blessed with the birth of our first son Matthew, followed fifteen months later by our daughter Melanie, and followed twenty-six months later by our son Andrew. We had climbed together to the top of the peak, breathing the clear mountain air, and praising God for the beautiful vistas around us.

Tim discovered knots and lumps on his neck about seven months after Andrew was born. It was during the Thanksgiving holidays, and our family physician gave him antibiotics as well as his home phone number in case Tim began to feel worse. I felt my breathing become shallow with every new concern. What followed was a biopsy of his neck, which revealed that Tim had Hodgkin's disease. Tim endured a grueling process that included scans, injected dyes, multiple doctor and hospital visits, bone marrow tests, and a staging laparotomy where they removed Tim's spleen and biopsied his liver to determine the extent of the Hodgkin's disease. I struggled to draw in a full breath with each new day.

Tim and our young family weathered the next yearlong, stony, and awkward path. It included six months of chemotherapy and six months of radiation treatments, followed by sixteen months of waiting and hoping to hear the word remission. Tim's blood counts were still abnormal. Thousands of dollars of blood testing, including more bone marrow testing, revealed a condition known as pre-leukemia or myelodysplastic syndrome (MDS). This dreaded unknown led to wondering daily what might lay ahead in the rocky bottomland of this arduous journey and more labored breathing as I understood the potential gravity of this syndrome.

They placed Tim on the registry to receive a donor bone marrow, and one year later he developed chronic myelocytic leukemia (CML or CGL), a condition assumed to be precipitated by previous chemotherapy and radiation. We were warned that his condition might not respond well to any further treatments. All our vistas disappeared in a brief moment of time.

Tim was instructed to spend a lovely weekend with his family and to return to the hospital on Memorial Day to begin the process of in-patient treatment, a difficult decision that could encompass more chemotherapy or radiation and a possible bone marrow transplant. I began to feel choked with the enormity of the task before us. Tim was in the hospital from May 31st until that fateful day, September 18, 1993 (111 hospital days), when I was called to the phone early in the morning with the dreaded news that Tim had experienced an episode of bleeding during the night. He had been blessed to receive more radiation, to receive donated bone marrow from some kind stranger, and to begin the process of the six-to-twelve weeks of recovery. The doctor who called that Saturday morning explained to me that the bone marrow transplant had not worked. It was a time when most recovering transplant patients succumbed to infection or to bleeding. Tim had suffered an irreversible bleed in his head, and I began to feel suffocated as I went to his side. I drove to the hospital and entered the room to join my husband. His nurse spoke softly to Tim, saying: "Your wife is here." With eyes half closed, Tim turned his head slightly toward the door and reached out his hand for mine. I grasped my husband's hand, he shook and squeezed mine gently, and we said goodbye.

I headed home to my children (ages seven, six, and four) and sat them down in the middle of the bed Tim and I had shared for eleven years. I gently reminded them their father had been sick for so very long, and told them he had reached the point where he could fight the illness no longer and had died. Their faces were filled with shock, disbelief, confusion, and sadness. Andrew, the youngest, seemed to understand the brevity of this news before anyone else as he cried out, "NO!"

Family began to circle around the four of us for support. We had a lovely memorial service, and the church filled to overflowing with family and friends. Tim had been a police officer and chaplain serving the law enforcement community, and other policemen and chaplains from surrounding communities came to pay their final respects. Their blue uniformed and stately presence lined the streets as we drove up; their salutes, show of support as they lined the walls of the church sanctuary, and white glove ceremony at the end of the service was such a comfort. In the days, weeks, months, and years that followed, we were surrounded by relatives, by church family and friends, and by the policemen who had loved Tim so dearly.

*Blessed be the God and Father of our Lord Jesus Christ, the Father of
mercies and God of all comfort, who comforts us in all our affliction,
so that we may be able to comfort those who are in any affliction,
with the comfort with which we ourselves are comforted by God.
Corinthians 1:3-4 (ESV)*

In the end, my rock bottom experience led to a renewed mountaintop
experience. God is gracious and merciful. He loves the widow and the orphan,
and comforts us in all our troubles. I learned three important lessons through
the untimely death of my dear Tim, lessons that often carry my weary soul to
the mountaintop. First, I learned to trust God with every breath I take. I would
wake in those early dawn mornings, remembering his death, feeling at rock
bottom again (as if for the first shocking time), suffering with the weight of the
realization that, on this earth, I would not see Tim again, and wondering how I
had even breathed enough times to survive another day. Breathing no longer
seemed a voluntary response, but a calculated chore.

Second, I learned to be grateful toward others and for what God had
provided. For me, the place of turning toward ultimate healing, of
reconciling this devastating loss as part of my new life, began with finally
becoming more grateful for the short time Tim and I had together, rather
than being disappointed and angry because of the time we would not grow
and share together.

Third, I learned to allow myself and others to grieve well—"our way"—and in a
way that even through indescribable pain, brought healing and strength and
led to helping others on similar journeys. I hoped this concept was remotely
possible. I purposefully planned toward it and plotted a course for it, knowing
that our three children depended on me to find a path that would lead
with surer footing to the top of the mountain—to learning to breathe again
without Tim, and to learning to depend on God more than we had depended
on our earthly husband and father.

I still have fears—fear of intense and inhumane suffering, fear of extended
and extreme illness, and fear of having to make those monumental medical
decisions again for myself or for those I love. I don't think I fear death, for to
die is to be reunited with loved ones again. To die (as my Mamaw said), is to
know that God is ready for you to leave earth, to hope and believe that He is

pleased with your service here, and to live in the presence of Christ for eternity, being loved, and worshipping with full joy.

I love the mountaintop, but I also know that rock bottom can be a beautiful place of immeasurable blessing, because there, too, God was present, powerful, and my protection. I felt His presence as if wrapped in a warm comforter. I felt at peace, with a peace that surpassed human understanding, and I knew the Lord was with us and would carry my little family along the path of this tragically beautiful journey called mourning. He led me all the way through the rocky and treacherous pass to a reconciling healing and toward being whole.

And in this wholeness, I would again be able to breathe freely and deeply of the crisp and clear mountaintop air.

Karen Lindwall-Bourg is the founder of RHEMA Counseling Associates, a biblical counseling, coaching, and training center that seeks to honor the Lord by leading others to the Sovereign God, the cross and life of Jesus Christ, empowerment by the Holy Spirit, and equipped with the Sufficient Word [Greek: rhema] of God for abundant life and ministry. Karen lives with her husband, Fred, in north central Texas and spends as much time as possible with their six children, five grandchildren, extended family, and a menagerie of ranch animals. You can find out more about RHEMA Counseling Associates at www.rhemacounseling.com.

ROCK BOTTOM IS A BEAUTIFUL PLACE

My Mother, Myself

God uses broken things. It takes broken soil to produce a crop, broken clouds to give rain, broken grain to give bread, broken bread to give strength. It is the broken alabaster box that gives forth perfume. It is Peter, weeping bitterly, who returns to greater power than ever. – Vance Havner

Hanne Moon

I leaned my head against the back of the chair and closed my eyes. Days had turned into weeks, but now the hours were counting down into minutes and seconds. My mother had been in ICU for a month, fever-ravished, infection-ridden, and vegetative. There was nothing more that could be done for her, and I knew the end was near.

I wanted to cry, but couldn't. Our relationship had been too fraught with rancorous volatility. There was hurt, frustration, anger, and a gradual disassociation through the years. I couldn't handle her rejection. She couldn't handle my independence. We were drawn to each other as moths to a flame, and how we burned in the presence of each other.

My parents adopted me from the American Embassy Hospital in Beirut, Lebanon when I was a baby. I actually have some pretty good memories of my mother during my life at home. Looking back, I can see the ways she wanted to be my friend. However, as I began growing older and needing my space, I began to keep her at arm's length. Most mothers understand this growing up and away of their children, but mine really didn't. She treated it as a rejection of her, which affected our relationship in so many ways.

Then my dad retired from the Army, got into a disastrous business arrangement with a family member, and eventually had to leave home, looking for work. We couldn't move with him this time, and I was left with my mother and my brother. I didn't know what was wrong with her during those months when she would do the most outlandish things. For example, she would begin cleaning out a fish tank (we had five of them, all twenty gallons and up), and before I knew it, she had all of them dismantled. She'd then lose focus and move on to "cleaning" up something else, moving through the house like a storm-force wind. I would stay up all night, trying to contain the wake of her hurricane antics. Along with all this, I was still trying to maintain a decent average in school, but failing miserably.

Somewhere in these years I became a Christian. It was only my church that salvaged my sanity during those years my father was gone. How do I explain coming home to a woman who was nearly catatonic, mumbling about events that happened years ago and which to her, seemed as only yesterday? These spells would pass and it would be as if nothing had happened. Only later did I find out that she had quit taking her Valium and anti-depressants during this time, flushing them all down the commode one day after years of high-dosage use. It took her months before she eventually overcame the withdrawal symptoms and life reverted back to whatever "normal" was for us. I tried to do the best I could and never told anyone of these episodes, not even my dad when he came home periodically.

We moved yet again, this time to Mississippi, where we eventually put down roots. It was here that I met my husband, whom she immediately hated. I'll never forget her words to me when I called her up to tell her I was getting married.

"We can't afford it."

I told her I wasn't asking her to pay for it and slammed down the phone. She eventually came around a bit to at least help me find a dress, although grudgingly, but it was a moment that began to define the rest of our years as mother and daughter.

I won't lie…I could never really understand her and my resentment of her grew more and more. It seemed she went out of her way to deliberately hurt me, and I pulled further and further away from her. One poignant memory is of me standing in the den in her house, several years after my father had died from the cancer he had contracted from Agent Orange during the Vietnam War, clutching the display case of his Army medals that I had made for him one Christmas. I remembered him crying when he'd opened it, because his time in the military had meant so much to him.

That day, I had stopped by her house to pick something up and noticed it on the floor, and I asked her why it wasn't on the wall where it usually hung. I picked it up, remembering in great detail 4 a.m. coffee with my father as we sat quietly across the table from each other before he headed off to work. I remembered helping him polish each piece of brass that was displayed behind the glass.

"I'm giving it to your brother," she said.

My head snapped up. "You'd give it to him without asking me first if I wanted it?" I was incredulous; I simply couldn't believe it. I had spent so much time and effort to put it together. I had even asked if she or my brother wanted to jointly give it to my father, and both had said no.

"It needs to stay in the family," she said.

"What am I? Chopped liver?"

"You know what I mean…I mean *real* family. Blood family."

I can't describe the ice that settled in my stomach at that statement, but a door closed in my heart for her that day.

My mother died without ever regaining consciousness, and as she rejected me in life, she rejected me in death. Out of the love and respect I had for my father and his memory, and the love he had for her, I spent another month cleaning up her belongings and packing her things away to be given to charity and whoever else she had designated them to.

But at the end of that time, I was through. I had never had such hatred in my heart for another person. For over four years I raged and I cried—at life, at circumstances I found myself in, at God. I was so angry that it was amazing I didn't burn my family and myself up in the flames of that hatred. There was no reasoning with me anymore. Forty-five years of hurt and anguish had festered and burst loose, and I could no more contain the oozing mess than I could contain a volcano.

Eventually, I burned out. All flames consume their source and die. I had been consumed. My soul and my heart were gone. I was an empty husk, and I had no desire for life or for God. I was a robot. Had it not been for my children and husband, and the fact that I could not desert them, I would have gotten into my car and left my life as I had known it, and never looked back.

At that point I simply pretended I never had a mother. I just didn't acknowledge her. Every picture I had of her was boxed up and put into storage. I allowed not one item of hers to be in my presence. When a friend of hers offered me a remembrance of her, I could not be gracious and accept it. I brusquely told her to keep it for herself, that it would be better served with her than with me.

As time went on, I began not to feel so empty anymore. I found the capacity to laugh and enjoy life. I was able to reach out to God again and accept that His gracious love for me had never left. They were little steps—little baby steps—but steps in the right direction all the same.

I was cleaning the kitchen one day and I recalled a story my mother had told me. She was from Denmark and had lived through the Nazi occupation of her country. Her father and stepfather were both members of the underground, which put her family in grave jeopardy. She told me of raids at the family home when she was but six or seven, and the Nazi soldiers pointing their rifles at her and her brother. And then another memory came to mind, of another story that she told me, a story of her family and alcoholism and meanness and actions of drunks that she had never forgotten. I thought of her bouts with depression and her years of Valium and anti-depressant use.

I stopped washing dishes for a moment and just sighed heavily. "My mother was so broken, God. Please, have mercy on her and just hold her in Your loving arms." I could no longer carry the burden of hating her. I no longer wanted to carry that burden.

The words He whispered to me tore through every wall I had erected. "My daughter, you're all broken. Each and every one of you."

I cried then…unfettered tears that would not stop. They washed away all the ashes of the burnt out husk that had remained of the inferno I had become. I sat at rock bottom of the pit I was in, and the only place to look was up.

My mother was not the final word on who I was. Her own demons colored her life as surely as mine embroidered a mural across the tapestry of mine. I realized my worth was not predicated on who I was when, how others perceived me, or the successes or failures in my life. My worth was tallied in every drop of blood that was shed on the cross.

And I was no more valuable than my mother was, not to God.

And she had been no more broken than I had become.

Our heavenly Father loves each and every one of us, and in that moment of revelation and since, He has allowed me the grace of being able to once more love my mother with the love He has for us. He has shown me time and time again, since that day, that He measures our worth as far as the east is from the west…

…from one scarred hand to the other.

Hanne Moon is a freelance writer, editor, and independent publisher of quality non-fiction and fiction through her publishing company, Heritage Press Publications. She has an avid love of the written word and enjoys helping writers find their voices. A self-confessed book addict, chocolate lover, coffee snob, and Jesus follower, she divides her time between work, family life, her vegetable garden, chickens, dogs, and grandchildren, all on twenty-seven acres in Mississippi.

Secrets in the Shade

In the long run, we shape our lives, and we shape ourselves. And the choices we make are ultimately our own responsibility. – Eleanor Roosevelt

Mel Ann Morales

"Will you have sex with my husband?"

It was a defining moment. This is not the moment that defines who I am as a human being, but the one that sheds a harsh light on my path to rock bottom.

I didn't ask the question—I answered it, with the way wrong answer of "yes." What my friend didn't know in that moment was that I had already had sex with her husband numerous times before she asked me to. He manipulated her into coming up with the idea, but the idea was all his because he didn't want to sneak around. I probably do not have to tell you that it ended badly.

This is where I struggle with my story. I left out a lot of details because they are a veiled attempt to justify what has happened and clothe the naked truth of just how ugly I really was. Mold hates sunshine, and I desperately want to find some shade rather than discuss this issue.

Three months earlier, I had dinner with the same friend. It had been over a year since I had even seen her husband. He told her to tell me "hello" and that he missed me. It was his veiled invitation, cloaked enough it got past his messenger, but obvious enough he knew I would RSVP.

When I got home that night, he contacted me. One short message. I gave one short reply. He gave a bit longer reply. It was game on. I matched his wager and raised him one. One message led to another, to another, to another.

Stop. If you didn't smell the stink on that last sentence, you should. It was a lie. Is it hot in here to you? That mold is searching for shade again.

Things just didn't lead to the next things. They rarely do. Every response… every answer to every question…every message, joke, vulnerability, and innuendo was carefully articulated and orchestrated to manipulate him. He was easy prey. My strategy was flawless. Just get him to a casual meeting face to face. Once that took place, nature would take over. It did. It went on for months. Did I mention that it ended badly?

In the interest of sunshine, let me be very clear on a subject most women won't even talk about. I am over forty. I love sensual sex. I have a libido that rivals the sex drives of most men. In the right context, that is extremely healthy and nothing to be ashamed of. That is, if it were to stop there.

When I say, "sex addict," what comes to mind? Porn? One night stands, lots of random strangers, hundreds of sexual partners by the age of forty?

I am a sex addict.

Here's the shade I have hidden under: Random strangers have always been a turnoff. There were way too many possibilities of disappointment. My total number of sexual partners is pretty low because I limited encounters with the same men that I found trust and chemistry and sensuality with. It was easy for me to believe that I was NOT a sex addict. Until I googled it and discovered that I am the typical female sex addict in one key area: Power.

Let that high noon sunshine brightly illuminate my sex addiction: It is not about the sex. It is about the power. Sex is the necessary means to that end. I orchestrated everything from beginning to end. The key was allowing him to believe he was in control. Control was not my thing. Control breeds unwilling slaves. True power, on the other hand, invokes voluntary servitude.

I often profess to being the heroine of my own story. I am also a dragon slayer. I have slain friendships, marriages, and families. I have played the villain in the stories of men. It is my unhealthy attempt at coping with powerless outcomes, out of fear of losing power without my consent. It became evident that I kept coming up empty and void of any real power outside of the moment. I learned that I cycle when I feel powerless in any area of my life. For example, the sudden loss of my dad triggered my last cycle.

In 2013, I went through something that left me feeling desperately powerless. My life was under a microscope. Turning to my addiction to gain any sense of power in my life was not an option. I discovered power within. I endured and created the outcome I desired, one I was told would be impossible. I walked away with that "impossible" outcome. Still not officially out from under the microscope, my grasp at the last straw for power was dying my hair blonde and bright violet. I felt as though my hair was the only thing left in my life that I had any control over.

Purple hair is not the worst ending to a powerless experience.

My fear in telling you this is that I will be judged unfit as a friend, partner, daughter, or mom. I also fear that men who learn this about me will try to exploit my weakness. My biggest fear is that I will feel less powerful.

My rock bottom was when I surrendered my power to a man with better skills of manipulation than I have. I nearly choked when I had to admit defeat to my mirror! For the first time in my life, I was played like a violin. It took a skilled sociopath to administer the poison. I got a good dose of what the other side of my addiction felt like. It was the day that I learned my friend's husband had been in love with someone else all along. He knew the only way his family would accept her was if he had someone else they could blame for the break-up of his marriage. Just because I didn't like being his instrument, doesn't mean I can say it wasn't well played.

I privately sought help with a sexual therapist that I have worked with privately for three years that no one (until now) knows I have been working with. I also have a small group of women I connect with weekly who have the same issues and we work through the 12-Step Program for Addicts. Privately, I have attempted to make amends with those whose lives were devastated due to my behavior. The most difficult conversation I ever had was meeting with my former friend and telling her all of the ugly truth about how she was manipulated by both her soon-to-be ex-husband and myself. I haven't found much forgiveness. I accept what I cannot change. But telling everyone I know and don't know that I am a sex addict? This is a new and scary experience for me.

Since my rock bottom realization, I discovered the secret that set me free. I tried old habits on a guy I met who politely shoved it down my throat for breakfast! He then taught me that some people in this world could be trusted rather than manipulated. He is now my best friend. He provides lots of sunshine for my mold. After that, I never attempted manipulation with him or anyone else. I found freedom and affirmation that comes from being in a relationship without manipulation!

I was raped when I was nineteen. This event left me feeling robbed of my power. So this was no surprise to my therapist that I tried to regain it through sexual manipulation of men. As far as relationships go, I craved intimacy. I wanted someone worthy of my trust. I discovered that power in healthy relationships is irrelevant if I make wise choices. I have found the more positive power of choice. It is what empowers a much better life.

I know that Rock Bottom is a beautiful place because it is the place where all "impossible" outcomes can become reality. It is where the beauty and healing power of grace shines brightest. It is the place where powerless living through addiction ended and my empowered life began.

Mel Ann Morales is an Empowerment and L.I.F.E. Tactical Coach who has mastered the art of playing with rocks and manipulating the space between a rock and a hard place! She is passionate about teaching women that they have the power to create the lives they desire—even in the midst of great crisis and loss—by developing the strategy of integrating daily practice of positive habits into a lifestyle of excellence. Mel Ann is also a homeschool mom to two beautiful children. http://melannmorales.com

ROCK BOTTOM IS A BEAUTIFUL PLACE

Release And Receive

Let all bitterness and wrath and anger and clamor and slander be put away from you, along with all malice. Be kind to one another, tenderhearted, forgiving one another, as God in Christ forgave you. – Ephesians 4:31-32 (ESV)

Melany Morrison

It was 1982, and our family was broken. I was a senior in high school and the oldest child of four. After years of family court, lawyers, judges, and those "trying to help," our family suffered a loss of income, increased verbal and physical violence, and fear. I missed my dad terribly when he left and longed for him to return.

My mom was mentally ill, but undiagnosed and without the correct prescription medications to control her illness. I believe she would be diagnosed today as Bipolar I with psychotic features. Growing up with her was rocky, and we nicknamed her Dr. Jekyll and Mr. Hyde. My father was a postman who didn't enjoy coming home to her because he was usually met with arguments and objects being thrown at him. Many nights when my parents fought, I would curl up under my covers in bed to hide. To this day, I still sleep with a blanket over my head. Screaming, banging, and doors slamming were nightly sounds my mother made.

As a child, teenager, and young adult, I was embarrassed of my mother, our dirty house, her appearance, and her constant smoking. I felt as if I could never let anyone come over and see the chaos at home or risk one of my mother's explosions. This shame, which I did not understand, carried on into adulthood.

When talk of divorce began, my mother's behavior became more and more out of control. The marriage ended many years before the actual divorce. My dad left many times and finally left for good in 1983, the year I was to graduate from high school. My mom was extremely angry at my father and soon began to take her anger out on me.

My mother's mood became unmanageable. One day, my dad picked me up after school and said I didn't have to ride the bus home. He took me to Dairy Queen and spent some time with me, talking and catching up. When I returned home, my mother saw that I had been with him and she became angry. I was trapped in my own home with my enraged mother. I finally escaped that horrible day at age seventeen, after she threw a lamp at me and attacked me with scissors. I left home for good with a black eye, bruises and cuts, a bloody shirt, a whole lot of shame, and not much else. At the time, I felt this was my rock bottom. I had nowhere to go but up.

I felt tremendous guilt for leaving my other three siblings behind. My mother begged me to come back home to help her case in the custody battle. My dad fought for all of us in court until she threatened to kill the boys. My father mysteriously dropped all efforts for custody of the children. She left Texas shortly after the case was settled and moved to California. I didn't speak to her for over six years.

I married my church sweetheart, who rescued me on that horrible day and helped me arrange a place to live with my church youth pastor and his wife until our marriage. I found solace in my faith, my husband's family, and my church. I cooked and cleaned and canned and quilted. We lived in the country north of Dallas, Texas, birthed two children, and had a great life. Soon, we migrated to Houston via Dallas, Waco, and Georgetown with every promotion my husband received.

While in Georgetown, I began to sell Discovery toys as a stay-at-home mom. While I had never run a business, traveled much, or met people outside my religious faith or culture, I was successful in recruiting other moms and built my team to over 300 ladies. I was traveling, training my team, going all over the world with incentive trips, and given many speaking and training opportunities. At the height of my career, my top salesperson and manager committed suicide. It was so unexpected because she was a top performer. I will never know why she abandoned her family in the worst way possible.

This threw me into a deep year-long depression. I asked myself "why" over and over, explored my own guilt, tried to make sense of it all, and shame reared it's ugly head once again. Did I cause this? Did I put too much pressure on her to sell? Could I have prevented this? Why didn't she share her secret? So many unanswered questions. Now this felt like rock bottom. How could I ever be able to motivate my team again? The shame prevented me from being able to look anyone in the eye. I felt incredible guilt and responsibility for her suicide.

It was at this time I decided to go back to school because I wanted answers. I also wanted to keep children from experiencing the pain I felt growing up. In my mind, the best way to do that was to become trained as a marriage and family therapist. The most important thing to me, after all, was my marriage and family. I wanted to teach couples to communicate and keep families together. I also had a deep desire to understand depression and anxiety so that I could help not only myself, but the millions of others who suffer with these mental disorders.

I was quite anxious about returning to school as an adult. My father was disappointed when I told him I wanted to be a marriage and family therapist. He said, "Your mom and I tried it, and it didn't work!" Despite his reservations, however, I was determined to continue. I did have the full support of my husband and eventually my father too.

Halfway through graduate school, we celebrated our twentieth wedding anniversary. My husband went all out. He took me to a jazz club downtown, gave me pearls, and sent flowers to the clinic where I had started seeing clients. On our date, we shared our deepest feelings about our marriage, and our hopes and dreams for the future. We discussed our regrets and how we overcame obstacles together.

Two days after that special date, he dropped dead of a massive heart attack. I had two teenagers to raise, to teach how to drive, and to send off to college. I was still in school and not yet working. I had never lived alone or held anything other than a part-time job. I was terrified! I became angry at God, which spilled into anger toward everyone I encountered. I lost many friends due to my anger. Even my mother-in-law stopped speaking to me, and I felt very alone.

When my children went off to college, I thought I would die from empty nest syndrome. I had read about it and thought I knew what to do, but I was not prepared for the utter emptiness I felt when my role as a mother changed. I just simply worked more and avoided coming home. It was too much of a reminder of what I had lost. Even the family dog died that year. I felt like I'd hit rock bottom yet again. Loneliness set in like I'd never known before.

It took getting to that lonely place to realize I needed help and, ultimately, needed God back in my life. Thankfully, several of my friends encouraged me to attend events and meet new people. I found the women of NACWE to be a great resource and example of love, encouragement, and ambition. I found God was there all the time, just waiting for me to return. When I released my anger toward God, I received the answer to my fears. I began to receive a love that can be shared with others, especially those cut off from us.

I believe there is nothing more painful in life than to be cut off from loved ones, to disappear from their lives. Shame reared its ugly head once again. I was ashamed I had turned my back on God.

Release…and receive…

I was sitting at a juice counter when the man making my juice voiced that phrase. I realized I was holding on to anger like a timid child holding onto the monkey bars on the playground. I was holding on for dear life!

The song that plays over and over in my head is from the movie, *Frozen*, "Let it go, let it go, let it go…" Why am I hanging on to anger? Why did I stop loving? I decided then and there that anger was keeping me at rock bottom and I needed to return to God, to allow Love to fill me so that I could truly love others again. I thought the anger I held onto for years just padded me and coated me with protection, but it was only when I pulled back the layers that I actually saw the core of who I was. There was a void that could only be filled with true Love, which is God. I wanted only to be accepted and loved the way God loves us.

I couldn't have done this alone. I had to ask for help during my despair. Suddenly, people began showing up out of nowhere! I still have broken family relationships and I long for repair and healing. The shame I once felt is now channeled into prayer and meditation. I pray for them daily and have hope that, one day, healing will take place. My calling and passion in life is to encourage others to repair broken relationships, to mend broken hearts, and to learn to ask for help.

Release...and receive!

Melany Morrison, LMFT, LPC, CGP, CART, is a licensed marriage and family therapist specializing in individual, couples, and family therapy, and maintains a private practice in Spring, Texas. In addition to being a prominent relationship therapist, Melany is an active Toastmaster and member of the National Speaker's Academy in Houston, Texas, speaking on a wide variety of topics. Melany loves to hike, cycle, travel to new places, and be outdoors. www.melanymorrison.com

ROCK BOTTOM IS A BEAUTIFUL PLACE

Rise Up! From Worthless to Priceless

He who began a good work in you will carry it on to completion until the day of Christ Jesus. – Philippians 1:6 (NIV)

Judi G. Reid

"I will hate you for the rest of my life, and I'm sorry you were ever born!"

As I write these words, even after hearing them more than fifteen years ago, I wish I could tell you they don't still sting. They do.

I had driven eighty miles to spend the weekend with my ailing mother. She wanted a reprieve from the nurse's aides on Mother's Day, which was also her eightieth birthday. It meant we could share mother-daughter time together. Alone. On the Sunday afternoon after the celebration, my mother suddenly glared at me and spewed her condemnation. As you can imagine, this verbal attack was not her first in my fifty-five years, but it hurt like a knife stabbing me in the gut. Essentially, she told me to leave. I had to accept the reality that those might have been the last words I'd ever hear from her before she died from her lung disease.

My prayer soon became, "Lord, please put her in a situation where she will have to see and need me, where I can show her love."

How could I utter such a prayer? Over the past ten years I had learned to no longer base my value on my mother's or anyone else's perception of me. According to John 1:12, I was confirmed as a child of God. I was *His* daughter.

Although her words may not have been the same when I was growing up, the atmosphere, attitude, and treatment prevailed most days and nights: rejection, ridicule, and a feeling of worthlessness.

As a teenager, I hit rock bottom. Unnoticed by my parents, I was already hanging out with a rough crowd. At the same time, I failed at playing the role of their proper daughter in a socially-elite circle. One night, I found myself trapped in a car on a date at a drive-in movie theater. The film was XXX-rated.

This experience added shame and guilt to my already damaged self-image. Instead of serving as a wake-up call, it opened the door to more experiences without boundaries. The picture of myself in the mirror, in my heart, and in my head seemed to confirm I deserved the disrespect and degradation I received. I often contemplated taking my own life.

After four rocky years of college, I married and had two children. To the outside world my life seemed perfect.

One weekend I attended a church conference for caregivers, where I met Pat Self. I'm convinced God placed her there just for me. My motive for going was jealousy. She had been invited to be the speaker when I thought it should have been me. I was the long-distance caregiver. I was the expert.

Well, I was wrong.

It didn't take long for me to understand why Pat had been chosen. She was an expert on caregiving, but more importantly, she was a woman of the Word. I definitely was not, nor did I desire to be. I feared becoming a "Jesus freak."

Without knowing my past, Pat told me how beautiful and priceless I was in God's eyes. She and I began to meet often for lunch. On one occasion, she said, "Judi, you're always trying to encourage others. How would you describe your own life?" I had learned to trust her and her relationship with the Lord. Although I didn't understand at the time it was the Holy Spirit, she had "something special." I wanted it too. She seemed to be able to penetrate though my usual happy face and smiles around others. So, I confessed. "I'm miserable, empty, and struggling for purpose to my life. I feel like my family would be better off without me."

That day, the dam began to crack. Living Water slowly flushed out the past and began to raise me up. She suggested a Christian counselor who understood post-traumatic stress disorder and the effects of pornography on a woman and her family. I continued to renew my mind with Philippians 4:8 images: *Whatever is true, whatever is noble, whatever is right, whatever is pure, whatever is lovely, whatever is admirable—if anything is excellent or praiseworthy—think about such things.* God has graced us with wonders to see, hear, taste and experience. These blessings had been there all along. I needed to view my life with new eyes and a new heart.

Pat urged my family to switch from our spiritually dead church that worshiped and recited prayers mechanically. We followed her advice, and I discovered the outrageous joy of worshiping freely—hands raised high, body swaying, clapping in fellowship with warm, caring, nonjudgmental people.

I joined the choir, attended women's Bible study, and participated in Christmas and Easter productions. I confess, I feared being viewed as a hypocrite, professing to be a Christian with a history of bad girl behavior. I accepted that, while I was in front of the congregation, singing and praising my little heart out, I was only able to do so because Jesus was living in me. I wasn't meant to hide under a bushel, isolated in shame. In His strength, I was an overcomer, in spite of my mistakes and weaknesses.

On my fiftieth birthday, I was baptized. I'm sure I shocked everyone when I proclaimed healing from a lifetime of thoughts of suicide. The redhead they saw as abundantly joyful had shared who she really was—or had been. Was I afraid? Oh, yes. At the same time, it gave me sweet release. It empowered me to connect authentically through my story.

I had emerged by accepting God's forgiveness. I met with a good Christian counselor and stayed in relationship with Pat and other godly women. I committed to daily devotions with the Lord and kept a journal. I intentionally avoided television. By applying Philippians 4:8, I decontaminated my home. In spite of a hereditary, incurable lung disease, I maintained a healthy lifestyle. I reached out to serve others and prioritized providing value to my children.

I believe God has always had a purpose for me in His plan. I went from struggling at rock bottom in the first third of my life to being set free into a life of joy. He uses my lifetime of hypersensitivity to rejection and sexual trauma as a voice for women. I hear Jesus calling me to raise them up to see their value in His eyes.

God has allowed me—always for good, though sometimes at the risk of pushing me back down into despair—to be an advocate. Issues that threaten our respect and dignity range from sex trafficking, immorality in media, pornography, cultural acceptance of inappropriate businesses in neighborhoods, to life in our own homes.

He uses me as an author. At age seventy, I published my first book, *Rise Up! 71 Thoughts of Hope and Inspiration for Women of Value*.

I am a Certified Life Coach and founder of Women of Value. Although my health necessitates restrictions, I focus on what I can do. Create. Promote. Empower. Serve.

God is faithful in all things. I will always remember how He answered my prayer for the end-of-life with my mother.

In August, after she attacked me on Mother's Day, I spent ten days on a mission trip in Romania with a women's ministry team. God opened the door to share my story through a Christian radio broadcast with expansive coverage to neighboring countries. That experience enhanced my healing and strength. In the meantime, my mother refused to take any calls from me.

Two months after I returned from Romania, I received a call from one of her nurse's aides. "Just as a precaution, we're sending your mother to the hospital. It's not an emergency," she said. I drove the eighty miles again. She needed me to advocate for her care in that public setting I'd prayed for. I was armed with her power of attorney, and she accepted my new role.

Eight days later, an ambulance transported her to a nursing home seven miles from my home. As the paramedics rolled her out of the back, she again glared at me and said, "I hate you." This time, I could respond with, "I love you,

Mother." In that moment, the legacies of abuse, suicide, and the stronghold of unforgiveness were shattered. Three days later, I lay at her feet as she took her last breath.

God took the hard rocks at the bottom of my pit and stacked them up high, creating something beautiful for His glory. This was a testimony for His Kingdom to His women of value.

Judi G. Reid is the founder of Women of Value. As an author, advocate and coach, she empowers women to "Rise Up! From your past, above your circumstances, into a new life of joy." You can visit Judi's website at www.WomenofValue.org or connect with her on Facebook at www. facebook.com/JudiGReid.

ROCK BOTTOM IS A BEAUTIFUL PLACE

The Latte (White) Lady in Africa

Trust in him at all times; pour out your heart before him. – Psalm 62:8

Denise Roe

I'm sitting here on Easter Sunday, knowing God can resurrect the dead and proclaiming My Redeemer lives! He is risen! I'm reflecting on what it was like going to Kenya by myself when I hit rock bottom on my knees in Mombasa, Kenya nine months ago.

You see, I have a dream deep inside that drives me to make a difference in lives that keeps me going. The devil used every tactic to persuade me to quit, get discouraged, and give up.

For over two decades I have traveled and launched ministries and missions trips around the world to make a difference in the nations. It has been a journey, being a voice to heaven, interceding for Africa, and after years of intercession, prayer, and divine appointments, I set sail for my first trip to Kenya. God raised up a divine appointment on June 28, so I bought my ticket to arrive in Kenya three weeks later on July 24 to speak at a pastor's conference. It was incredible sharing with hundreds of pastors and leaders about John 3:2 and a missions marketplace movement coming to Africa through the healthy coffee that pays.

After three weeks of travel in Kenya, staying in homes, hotels, and guesthouses, I had a total of four hot showers. Someone said that is good that I had that many! I guess it's a matter of perspective. I learned how to take sponge baths and then heat water in a kettle to take warm sponge baths. I was investing my savings to launch a business into Africa.

Then challenges came and opening the business was going to be delayed. Financial resources were dwindling and the town on the coast was not as expensive as Nairobi, so I took an all-night bus ride back to the coast. Besides, I would be able to see the beach again!

So there I was, by myself, without a spouse, waiting for the man of God's choice, and with no one from the United States traveling with me, staying at a guesthouse by myself. I missed the lesson from the locals and colleagues (as well as people on the ground) until after I got back home that I should not have been travelling alone. Apparently everyone thought someone else was with me. Thank God for protection and my warrior worship spirit that kept me safe. (Not to mention being a health strategist to adapt to the many environmental challenges, foods, and having my water machine break the night I arrived, that it was the grace of God I stayed healthy.) Thank you, Lord!

The longing in my heart to jog on the beach while praying and interceding for freedom to come to the people of Africa was energizing on the morning of August 21. Little did I know what I would encounter within the hour. I came back from a spiritual recharge to my locked hotel room, and when looking for my wallet to put the change in that I always carried with me on the walks for water, phone top up, or *matatu* (the little scooter transport), I realized my wallet was not in my purse. Where could it be? I looked around the room, stunned for a moment, and then wondered if it went missing the night before when I went to dinner. My mind was racing through the events of the night before, but as I reached for my iPhone, I realized it, too, was gone—and much more.

The laptop had been on the bed with the iPhone and MP3 player, plugged in for charging. Everything was gone. I immediately called the owner of the guesthouse to meet me, but he was in no hurry. Soon, the staff found out I had been robbed, but no one had the number to the police, and I knew that every minute was of the essence.

With no help or phone number, I walked to the police station, more like a storming march of "don't mess with this white lady." A colleague and pastor met me at the police station and after many hours of filing reports, we went to the guesthouse to inspect the location of the theft. It was then that I realized my iPad was also gone. I became upset at the loss of all my photos and memories, since I didn't have time to journal. I was thankful that I had tucked my passport inside a pocket in my purse and only the wallet was taken, however. So, now I had a Kenya phone and a U.S. passport. What more could a girl have asked for? (A man to accompany me, maybe?)

I began to think about cancelling my travel plans back to Nairobi the next day for the long awaited business meeting and just take a couple of days to enjoy the beach. Or I could just go home—I was done. It was August 21 and my ticket home was August 26. The big event with corporate staff was scheduled for August 22, but since I knew that the business wasn't going to open until October, I wasn't sure it really mattered that I go back into Nairobi city to attend. I sought counsel and decided to make the journey.

I made a phone call to see if someone could pick me up at the Nairobi bus station when I arrived with my two bags. They weren't sure and didn't understand how I had gotten out of Nairobi by myself.

It was at that moment I went off to the 'garden by the poolside" and thought of the garden of Gethsemane. I was wailing—a heart wrenching cry asking God what more did He want, what more could I give? There was nothing left … spiritually, emotionally, mentally, physically, and financially. I appeared to be a spiritually strong and successful single woman, but I felt so vulnerable. Empty. Alone. Nothing can aptly describe how I felt at that moment.

I was tired, emptied, exhausted, and had nothing left to give. I caught my breath after pouring out my heart to God. Within minutes, God sent a pastor and colleague to love on me and help me get me back into Nairobi for the meeting. After a nine-hour bus ride all night by myself, we pulled into the

Nairobi station. My Kenya phone battery was about to die. I sent texts to several people to be sure someone was there to pick me up, but I got no response. I was all alone again in the city with two large suitcases, being stared at by all. All eyes on the white lady.

I got a taxi and got out safely with my bags. I made it to the hotel and found some breakfast. It was several hours later before anyone asked my whereabouts. It was an incredibly difficult few days before flying home.

Once again, I felt incredibly vulnerable at the Nairobi airport that had suffered a major fire just two weeks prior. All the vendors were in tents, including money exchangers, phone, and security. I felt like a prostitute walking down the streets as hundreds of men looked at me. At times I could feel my insides shaking before I managed to get on the plane for the return trip home.

All I can think of (and say now) is thank you, God! I am safe and healthy. As I reflect on being so alone, I realize my heart is now open more than ever to meet the man of God's choice. I have known for many years that I'm not called to go to the nations alone and my heart has another layer unlocked to embrace that day when I will be married.

Will I go back to Africa? Absolutely. I will pray about the timing most of all and not go alone. There is a good probability that I will be back before this is published and be able to declare I know my Redeemer lives and will continue to use this white latte lady to impact the nations. I pray for the man of God's choice to partner with me and believe, but I know for now that I am not alone in pursuit of making a difference. It has been a hard nine months since I went to launch a business in Africa, and now God is bringing it forth. The season of birthing pains and learning to trust Him at all times was worth it!

I know my Redeemer lives and there is freedom from the shores of Africa to North America. A special thank you to Nicole C. Mullen, Tammy Trent, and Mandisa for life giving words on my prayer jogs. YOU ROCK! And you empowered me to rock the nations and change the atmosphere during intercession as I declare His destiny and purposes.

"Trust in him at all times; pour out your heart before him" (Psalm 62:8).

Worship while you war, wait, win and at all times!

I know my Redeemer lives! At all times!

Denise Roe is a health strategist, speaker, trainer, teacher, connector, and Toastmaster. She has launched businesses and charities globally and has travelled to twenty countries. She resides in the Dallas Metroplex with her cat of eighteen years where she built her home nine years ago. Denise has been an entrepreneur for twenty-five years and is passionate about making a difference in lives all over the world. As a health strategist, after her personal journey of looking for answers to prevent cancer, she identifies the "A-HA" moments in your health so you can fulfill your destiny. www.deniseroe.com

---

Finding the Courage to Heal

"If we are creating ourselves all the time, then it is never too late to begin creating the bodies we want instead of the ones we mistakenly assume we are stuck with."
– Deepak Chopra

Paula Tobey

Healthy for most is not healthy for me.

I have been suffering from migraines since I was twelve years old. My first one came when I was babysitting. I had to call my mom to come over and help because I was seeing stars and my head was pounding. I felt so nauseated, I could not stand. In college, the migraines got much worse and my aunt-in-law, a nurse, called a hospital in Boston and had me admitted. They diagnosed me with chronic migraines and prescribed pain medication and a preventative.

The medicine only brought me temporary relief, but because I felt the doctors knew what they were doing and I did not, I did as I was told and put up with the pain. For years, the cycle continued and the migraines persisted. One year at Thanksgiving, I was at my aunt and uncle's house in Pennsylvania and had to go to the emergency room because I could not stop getting sick. As a matter of fact, I got sick often from the headaches, even at my sister's wedding. But that was just how it was—my head liked to hurt. It was my way of life.

In college, I had a ski accident which resulted in a torn ligament. I wore a knee brace from my thigh down to my ankle. For years, I thought my torn ligament never properly healed, causing me intense pain. Years later, when my girls were born, I spent time trying to get healthier (more for them than for me). I then realized my knee pain was back, only it felt worse and it had mysteriously migrated. It hurt all the time. Luckily, I was always on some kind of pain killer and my knee pain was not as bad as it could have been. Although the pain woke me up most nights, it hurt less when I moved it. Many nights, I remember sitting on the couch with my knee up, rubbing on it, wishing I could get the pain to lessen. It was not ever swollen, even when I worked out. When I had doctors look at it, they said it was absolutely fine. *Fine,* huh? Well, thanks. I could only guess I was crazy.

After my second daughter arrived weighing a whopping ten pounds, I felt I'd earned a badge of honor for pushing her out of my petite five-foot one-inch frame. However, I noticed that one of the side effects after her birth was that I could no longer hold the urge to go to the bathroom. I figured that was normal after having such a big baby; little did I know, her size did not matter. My body ended up recovering just fine from her birth. The pain was another issue altogether.

As you can imagine with all of these unrelated health issues, my capacity to be a great mom diminished significantly with every pill I popped and each limping sprint to the john. The worst part was that I noticed my own irritability increasing. I yelled a lot and had terrible brain fog. My husband called home every evening to find out the state of affairs and to see if he was coming home to the two-headed dragon lady! The sad truth is *he was,* and I hated it. I hated who I was as a wife and a mother, and I often cried myself to sleep.

Every headache that left me parenting from the couch made me realize I needed help. My dreams of teaching again were diminishing. I was so sick all of the time and it made me miserable. However, I did what I knew to do: pretend

I was okay and swig down my concoction of over-the-counter and prescription pain pills. If someone asked how I was doing (because they could tell I had a screaming migraine from the look on my face), I would answer, "I'm here." I could not stop my life all the time just because my head was pounding like a jackhammer. What a way to live! I never really told anyone how much medicine I had to take just to make it through. I began praying to God that my issues were related and I could get *real* help. I felt like a drug addict and I worried people knew.

I finally decided I needed professional help. I knew I must have been depressed, especially by the way my husband responded to me—like I was another person, a *dragon lady*. So, I went to a counselor. I laid out all of my "problems," and she diligently took notes. My life was great: my marriage was good, our finances were good, and our kids were good. I worked part time at a health club, so I was regularly exercising. I just always felt awful. She told me she thought I had food issues. Well, how could that be? I ate pretty darn healthy. I knew junk could make you feel bad, but I did not eat a lot of junk. So, I left her that day denying help, even though she persisted. She thought I had food allergies.

One week later, I ate a sandwich from a local shop that changed my life forever. Within minutes of eating it, I got so sick it was coming from everywhere. It was ridiculously embarrassing! That night, the pain was unbearable. When I woke up the next day, (somehow still alive despite all the medicine I had taken trying to quench the pain), I was crying—no, *sobbing* on my knees to the Lord. Every single day I lived in pain, trying to hide my problem from the world. I put on that brave face every mom has to wear and carried on pretending I felt okay. Everything I was doing by myself to get better was not working. That day I realized I needed help from *Him* to get better. Not until then did I truly get relief.

A few days later, I went back to my counselor and said I was ready to do whatever she told me. I did not care what it cost; *I had* to feel better. My marriage depended on it, and my life with my kids meant too much to lose. I was at rock bottom and needed help. I was desperate. Thank *God* she was the right person I needed to see and she also happened to be a registered dietitian. Thank *you*, God!

After some counseling from her office, my dietitian and I worked together to create a healthier lifestyle for me and, eventually, my family. I had to go corn-, spinach-, gluten- and coffee-free. If you have ever read the package of any cereal, pasta, or chips, you realize that is no easy feat! The bigger problem was that I had to learn to cook from scratch, something I had not done much before. I had a lot to learn.

During this time, I relied a lot on my faith to get me through. I had to learn to do things differently, but I also knew since I was terrified, I was *supposed* to do them! God had saved me and He would sustain me. He showed me that in order to really be healthy, I needed to talk to Him and rely upon Him *daily*. Only then could I live a "PheMOMenal" life.

I learned from this experience that I really needed to go to my Heavenly Father sooner. Only *He* can heal me. For years, I believed the doctors would fix me. I believed I ate the right things. I thought the medicine would work. I thought I would have to live with migraines forever. I often thank the Lord He showed me a way to natural health. He educated me on a healthier way to live. I am one lucky mama! Because I hit rock bottom, I turned to Him for healing. Today I live joint pain-, IBS-, and migraine-free with no medicine, and *that* is a beautiful place to be.

Paula Tobey is a former teacher. When she began her business as a parent coach, she knew her mission to help children had to start by empowering and equipping their parents to be and do better. She knows from firsthand experience as a mom of two daughters that "if mama isn't happy, nobody's happy." She helps moms become healthy from the inside out as a Healthy Living Coach. For more information about Paula, visit www.phemomenallife.com.

19 Degrees To Change

Our deepest fear is not that we are inadequate. Our deepest fear is that we are powerful beyond measure. It is our light, not our darkness that most frightens us. We ask ourselves, who am I to be brilliant, gorgeous, talented, fabulous? Actually, who are you not to be? You are a child of God. Your playing small does not serve the world. There is nothing enlightened about shrinking so that other people won't feel insecure around you. We were born to make manifest the glory of God that is within us. And as we let our own light shine, we unconsciously give other people permission to do the same. As we are liberated from our own fear, our presence automatically liberates others. – Marianne Williamson

Kofi Williams

On December 15, 2008, it was nineteen degrees outside. Ice made it treacherous to drive and the wind cut right to my bones. My heart was heavier than usual during the three-hour drive back to Oklahoma City from my home state of Texas. I had spent the weekend with my 42-year-old baby sister and best friend, Teresa, who was losing her six-year battle with cancer. I wanted to capture every moment of our remaining time together and be strength to my family.

My sister was dying and so was my marriage. Before I'd left the previous Friday, things had continued to spiral downward between my husband and me. I feared losing my sister, as well as what awaited me back in Oklahoma City, anxious at the thought of facing my husband.

I exhaled a sigh of relief as the car slid onto the icy driveway. I pressed the garage remote, anticipating the familiar sound of the door lifting.

Nothing happened.

I tried the remote again, but still the garage door wouldn't budge. My heart beat faster as my breathing grew shallower. I made my way to our front door, inserted the key, and turned the knob. The door wouldn't open. Terrified, I called my husband's cell phone, but it went straight to voice mail. I called again and again, even trying his office. Not sure what to do or where to go, I sat in the driveway, turning on the rental car to keep warm as my heart sank. Since I'd only been in the state for ten months, I didn't know anyone well enough to ask for help. I didn't want my family to face the treacherous drive in the horrible weather. Besides, they were already burdened enough with my sister's terminal illness. I was stuck, feeling helpless.

I sat crying in the rental car for three hours before my husband finally called. I asked why he hadn't called me back until now.

"I have a business to run," he said coldly. "I can't just drop everything because you called." He told me his attorney had advised him to change the locks. He had started divorce proceedings.

"What am I supposed to do?" I asked.

"I'll take you to a hotel," he replied. "I don't care what you do after that."

"But I don't have a car, money, nothing! I'm your wife! Why do you act like you hate me?"

"What makes you think I'm acting?" he said coldly.

He drove me to a hotel on an unfamiliar side of town, paid for a week's stay, and left three hundred-dollar bills on the table. Terrified, I begged him not to leave me there as he turned and left. Several hours later, he returned with all my things in boxes, completely covering every inch of space in the small hotel room. As the door closed behind him, I surveyed the room, ashamed that at 48-years-old, my life was reduced to a hotel room full of my belongings, another failed relationship, abandoned in a city where I knew no one.

Only ten months before, I'd been on the white beaches of Maui at sunset having my dream wedding with the man I loved. For the past three decades, I'd battled clinical depression, searching for love in all the wrong ways, in all the wrong men. I finally had it all: my Prince Charming, a big house, cars, a boat and what was sure to be a great marriage. I now knew my Prince Charming was really a Dark Knight with emotional damage of his own.

After I stopped crying, I called a close friend in Texas who happened to be a life coach. I ranted about what he had done to me and what a terrible person he was. Finally, she said in a very soft voice, "Wow, he must be in a lot of pain to cause you that much pain. Hurt people hurt people."

I suddenly stopped crying and felt a calmness come over me, realizing the truth in her words. The common denominator in my life was not unhealthy relationships, but me. If I wanted my life to be different, then I had to first be different. That night, I asked God to deliver me from this rock bottom, praying, "God, please show me the way."

I had sold my car before leaving Texas; my husband had three vehicles and assured me I wouldn't need mine. I applied for a car loan weeks before leaving to visit my sister, not really believing that I would be approved. I knew having my own transportation would give me some form of added security as our relationship became unbearable. After three weeks, I hadn't heard from the lender.

The next day, I called my office and asked for a couple of days off while I figured out what to do. As I sat in my box-filled room feeling miserable, a small voice clearly said, "Do not be afraid. Call the lender." Still uncertain, I picked up the phone and called Carol, the loan officer.

"Oh, yes, Ms. Williams," she said. "Your loan was approved several weeks ago. It just got buried on my desk. I am so sorry!" My heart leapt with joy as I began to cry with relief. By the end of the day, I was driving my own car. God had heard my simple prayer and showed me His power.

A couple of days later, I received a call from a co-worker I had only met once, just long enough to discover a shared love of photography. She invited me to go on a photo shoot with her so she could show me around the city. Thinking it might help me feel better, I agreed.

Afterwards, we stopped for lunch. "I don't know you at all," she admitted. "But I sense something's wrong." I gave her an abbreviated version of my story as she listened intently. "Want to know how I got to Oklahoma from Chicago?" she asked. "I followed a guy out here. It didn't work out. He kicked me out of his apartment and I've been here ever since." She then took out her key ring, removed a key, and gently slid it across the table to me. "I live alone. I work a lot of hours. I have a three-bedroom house. We're getting you out of that hotel room today. I insist. You can stay with me as long as you like." In a mere three days, I went from being homeless and abandoned to having a new car and a safe place to live.

As the weeks progressed, there were many days I didn't think I could go on, but I didn't have the nerve not to. I knew I had beaten depression once and for all long ago. Though my life was in a dark place, I vowed not to go back to permanently living in that darkness.

I spent the next two years dedicated solely to working on me. Through prayer, coaching, meditation, and a tremendous amount of personal development, I evolved from a woman with low-self esteem to one who inspires and teaches others that just because you're hurt, it doesn't mean that you're broken and just because you aren't where you think you should be in life, it doesn't mean that you can't get there.

On April 26, 2011, my little sister made her transition. Because of my rock bottom experience, rather than falling apart, I was able to boldly stand before an overflowing church and give a eulogy that strengthened others. I know Teresa was proud of her big sister; it's what she would have done for me. That same year on her birthday, I became a certified professional life coach and created my business, 19Degrees2Change Personal Development, teaching women how to love and honor themselves.

Six years since my rock bottom experience, I'm now in a healthy, loving relationship with a man I will grow old with. He loves, protects, and adores me—history and all. Most importantly, rock bottom taught me to show myself the same love that God so generously gives.

In 2011, after thirty years of corporate experience, Kofi Williams became an entrepreneur and founded 19Degrees2Change Personal Development. She is a full-time trainer, coach, speaker, and facilitator. She specializes in helping women transform their lives through her Wake Up & Live! System, which teaches women to live by choice, not by chance, balance self-care with care for others, and distinguish between guilt and responsibility so that they live a life they love. With Kofi's guidance, women give themselves permission to discover who they are at their core, unlock their full potential, and begin living a life of purpose. More information about Kofi and her Wake Up & Live! programs can be found at www.19d2c.com.

A Beautiful Mind

Let this mind be in you, which was also in Christ Jesus.
– The Apostle Paul

J. Nicole Williamson

A beautiful mind is a beautiful thing, but a dark mind is a dreadful place to live. I have known both.

God's love, I've discovered, is the great transformer of ashes into radiant beauty. I've found it to be the divine energy needed for the upward lift to the wings of my inner man. It empowers my heart to soar like an eagle and to see from a higher perspective for overcoming life's battles. It is the absence of love, however, that acts like a vacuum, generating a dark force with a downward pull on the mind. Unchecked, it easily becomes a cyclonic effect of disturbing thoughts swirling violently in the soul as a fierce wind of inner destruction. I know this by experience.

From early on, I struggled with fears and a sense of personal worthlessness. I hadn't experienced any overt trauma, but I was quick to internalize every rejection, real or perceived, as my standard of truth. By the time I hit my mid-teens, self-rejection had spread its roots deep into my heart and entwined its branches around my mind, and my soul became a dark place.

Negative thinking grew, driving my emotions with continual conflict. I cursed myself often, a few times even cutting my body to vent feelings of self-disdain. I hated me and I was angry at the world, though I wasn't sure why. These things drew a dark presence into my life that enclosed me like a tangible prison.

Drugs and alcohol were my way of escape, but as my actions brought shame to my parents, it also added to my sense of guilt. After all, I was a Christian and I knew what I was doing was wrong. At sixteen I was convinced I should end my life and attempted to do so with my father's .45 revolver. Divine intervention and three weeks in the hospital fortunately altered my plan.

My journey from there took me through counseling, time in juvenile detention, five months in a reform home, and two years away from home under the care of a Christian ministry, including a year of Bible college. And yet, after all this, I felt no freer from my internal war with darkness. Counselors and pastors alike arrived at the same hopeless conclusion about me: no one seemed to know how to help me, or how to stop the conflicts that ravaged my mind.

My rock bottom place came when I had just turned twenty. I thought I had been at rock bottom many times before, only to find they had merely been hard landings on jagged ledges. I had moved back home ten months earlier and finished a second year of Bible college. I was still struggling with my addictions. It was late summer and I had just returned from a four-day Christian retreat near Spokane. I felt utterly broken inside and weary of my battle.

At the retreat, I knew I had come to the end of myself. From the first opening song to the concluding message, I wept. A deep fountain within me broke open; it was like an unstoppable flood. I wanted desperately to be whole, but I didn't know how, nor even what the root of my problem was. But God did. All I knew was that it was very dark inside my soul. I had tried every known means, good and bad, to find peace and freedom, but to no avail. Yet, in the midst of these tears, I felt as if the Holy Spirit's own intercession was mingling with the cries of my spirit as I reached desperately out to One I knew had the answer to my plight.

Back at my parents' home, I sat staring out the large kitchen window, barely noticing the scenic view of the Willamette Valley and majestic Mt. Jefferson in the distance. My thoughts were interrupted by a knock at the door. A pastor from Argentina and his wife had come to stay for a week while they ministered to various churches in the area. I look back today and know their arrival was God's answer to my cry. From the first moment, they saw the conflict that shrouded me and felt impressed to invite me to return to Argentina with them. Seeing a glimmer of hope for freedom, I went.

God knew when my heart was truly ready for change. He knew when I hit rock bottom—the place where I was willing to face truth, deal honestly with my issues, look to the Light, and be set free. It apparently took me a long time to get there!

Like Ruth in the Old Testament, I went to a land I didn't know, to a people I didn't know, and whose language I couldn't speak. However, I knew one thing: God was moving there. It was just prior to the famous revival under the ministry of Carlos Annacondia. Nevertheless, the ministry I was with was already in revival and known for the presence of God. They were called "the singing church." Services were held nearly every night, lasting from three to five hours long. My first service in Buenos Aires is etched deep in my memory. I was impacted as I watched the people worship. Their faces beamed as tears streamed down their cheeks, and I knew they were experiencing a glory I had not yet known. I wondered how I would ever come to know God in such depth and intimacy!

A few days later, I was taken south to Mar del Plata where Instituto Biblico Peniel became my home for the next three years. I lived with the students, though I didn't attend classes. When I wasn't working in the office or doing chores, I was in prayer or personal study. I had no television, radio, or outside influence to distract me from my purpose. It was as if God had placed me in a womb where He could heal my heart and put me together. He surrounded me with those who poured His love on me.

I was told that two important keys were needed for personal transformation: God's Word and presence. In the revival services, I experienced His strong presence. I learned as I watched others engage with the Holy Spirit through deep repentance, open prayers, declarations of surrender, incredible rejoicing, and passionate worship. I watched them war against any inward agreement with sin and darkness. They held nothing back, but came honestly, humbly, and wholeheartedly into God's presence—singing, dancing, lifting hands, with tears and laughter, all in unhindered expression of love for Jesus.

I had to learn to draw near to God, and so the Holy Spirit became my intimate Helper and Teacher. My daily time in the Word was dry at first, until He opened my understanding. Then it became a fountain of life that washed my soul. Two scriptures became my theme. The first was one that God gave to me— Jeremiah 29:13 (NIV): *"You will seek me and find me when you seek me with all your heart."* This not only became my lifeline of hope for change, but also my guide for intimacy with God. It was clear: I had to seek Him with all my heart. The second was Psalm 27:4 (KJV) and was my response to Him: *"One thing have I desired of the Lord, and that will I seek after, to behold the beauty of the Lord and to enquire in His temple."*

Breakthroughs came, but transformation was not overnight. It took time for my heart to soften, for darkness to break its grip, for love to take root and replace wrong thinking. It took time to learn the obedience of love, to both receive love and give it. God's presence drew me continually to Himself, teaching me my identity as His beloved daughter and Christ's cherished bride.

Months passed with deep searching, breaking strongholds, and drinking in His glory. Then came the unforgettable moment when Jesus appeared to me. I was simply worshipping and thanking Him for all He'd done, when there He was. I was with hundreds of people in a service, but in that moment there was no one in the room but Him and me. The chains I'd tried so desperately to break fell in His presence. I heard them shatter and I knew I was free. I knew I would never be the same.

It's been over thirty-five years since that day, and I've not stopped growing and walking as a free woman in Christ. The Father, Son, and Holy Spirit continue to mature me in His love as I savor the joy of being translated from the kingdom of darkness to the kingdom of light.

Today, I love my life, I know my value, and I know who I am. I also know my authority and purpose in God. I have a beautiful mind—Christ's mind that fills me with what is true, honest, pure, and lovely. I have learned to overcome darkness through the power of Jesus's glorious love, and to soar in life with a mind of hope on the wings of infinite grace.

J. Nicole Williamson is an inspirational author, speaker, and founder of King's Lantern International, a teaching ministry committed to empowering people in authentic identity and intimacy with God. Her books include, The Empowered Woman, The Esther Mandate, *and* Heaven's Secret of Success. *She and her husband live in the Dallas, Texas area. You can learn more about her teaching ministry at www. kingslantern.com.*

ROCK BOTTOM IS A BEAUTIFUL PLACE

Afterword

Are you amazed at the glory of God? His grace? His power? How He takes our broken pieces and uses every single one of them to help others?

My prayer is that you have been inspired by the real women who have shared their real stories. Real, authentic, gut-level, honest truth.

Women just like you.

Many of the women in here struggled with sharing their stories. These are not easy stories to read. They were even harder stories to write. But as they shared, as they wrestled with their words, with their insecurities, and with their fears, something amazing happened.

They were set free in so many ways.

We know that Rock Bottom is a beautiful place.

We know that we walk forward from here in the strength of God and our shared sisterhood in Christ.

We pray this over you and your story, that it will bring you closer to the God who loves you.

Prayer Of St. Francis

Lord make me a channel of thy peace—that where there is hatred, I may bring love—that where there is wrong, I may bring the spirit of forgiveness—that where there is discord, I may bring harmony—that where there is error, I may bring truth—that where there is doubt, I may bring faith—that where there is despair, I may bring hope—that where there are shadows, I may bring light—that where there is sadness, I may bring joy.

Lord, grant that I may seek rather to comfort than to be comforted—to understand, than to be understood—to love, than to be loved.

For it is by self-forgetting that one finds. It is by forgiving that one is forgiven. It is by dying that one awakens to Eternal Life. Amen.

God is good. We are delighted that you are with us on this journey, and we pray that you will consider joining us in the next Rock Bottom book. We believe that God is opening the door for this to be a series of books that share hope with the world!

We encourage you to reach out to us:

- www.rockbottomisabeautifulplace.com
- Visit each woman's website
- Friend them on Facebook

When you feel like you have hit the bottom, trust God.

Look up.

Ask for help.

Surrender.

Give Him your broken, empty, worn out heart. He is waiting for you and He loves you so very much!

You are beautiful in your brokenness.

About Diane Cunningham

Diane Cunningham, M.Ed. is the President and Founder of the National Association of Christian Women Entrepreneurs®, a global association where women meet to connect, create, and collaborate. NACWE offers training, conferences, networking, and business strategies. NACWE was launched in May 2010 and has been building and expanding since that time with members throughout the United States and Canada.

In 2014, she founded the Christian Women's Leadership Institute™ to train women to become Certified Group Facilitators and to raise up leaders around the world.

Diane is a "business therapist," plane crash survivor, author, consultant, speaker, marathon runner, and fun friend. She has a Master's Degree in Education (Guidance and Counseling) from Whitworth College in Spokane, Washington, as well as a Bachelor's Degree in Interpersonal Communications.

Diane is an Amazon Best-Selling author of *The Inspired Business Toolkit*, along with *Dear Female Entrepreneur, My Friend*. She also co-authored *Inspired Women Succeed* with Jo Ann Fore.

She currently lives in Grapevine, Texas where she drinks too much coffee, eats chips and salsa, and connects with friends as often as possible.

Diane's mission is this: To inspire women to dream big, catch on fire, and change the world.

Connect with Diane at www.facebook.com/DianeCunninghamFriends and www.facebook.com/NACWE for fun updates, silly videos, lively conversation, and great ACT FAST NOW business mentoring.

Email her at diane@dianecunningham.com and join us at www.nacwe.org.

Join our NACWE family!

Are you a woman who has the dream of starting a business?

Or a woman who has been successful in business, but lacks the support of a group of like-minded friends?

Are you a Christian entrepreneur tired of being alone with your standards, ethics, and values?

We know how you feel...

- Are you wondering where to begin?
- Fearful of asking for the sale?
- Do you struggle with social media?
- Are you totally overwhelmed with your list of to-do's?
- Struggling to figure out if you need to hire help and who to hire?
- Feeling isolated as you work alone or as the boss of a small group?

Or you might be...

- Undercharging for your services
- Overwhelmed by technology
- Afraid of being "salesy"
- Know you need a better system, but have no idea what that means

You have found the right place!

At NACWE, we "get it" and we "get you"! We get you because we are YOU!

The National Association of Christian Women Entrepreneurs was born out of a passion to connect women who are ready to create, collaborate, and contribute to changing the world. We gather people and ideas together through online content, tele-courses, individual/group coaching and retreats. Our desire is to unite under a common goal of helping one another to succeed and thrive in business. We are blessed to share in a common faith in Jesus Christ, and yet know that we might each choose to worship in a different way.

Get **connected** to Christian women entrepreneurs throughout the United States and Canada for networking, business building, and prayer support.

Start **creating** new ideas, plans, programs, and products with help from our valuable monthly training calls and webinars.

Begin **collaborating** with women who can walk beside you on the journey with love and not competition.

Visit us at www.nacwe.org to get started with your membership today!

Invite Diane to Speak

Inspiring Heart-Based Businesswomen To Infinite Success

Diane Cunningham is a gifted communicator who offers inspiration, motivation, and encouragement to all those who come into her path. Her genuine transparency comes through in the insightful examples she gives her audiences as she helps them to create a life filled with passion and purpose. She loves to provide inspiration strategies for business groups, weekend gatherings, or corporate retreats.

As a speaker, Diane facilitates interactive discussions, along with providing useful and thought-provoking information for seminars, networking events, and women's retreats in the church and corporate realm. She is also available for corporate training events and keynotes.

"Diane Cunningham is an engaging, enlightening, speaker. Her powerful, heartfelt message is full of substance, easily remembered, and when implemented, inspires women to a higher level of success. It is with the greatest of confidence that I recommend Diane Cunningham."
– Julie Ziglar Norman
Founder of Ziglar Women, *Guideposts* author, international inspirational speaker
www.ZiglarWomen.com

Diane speaks to groups of:

- Christian women in business
- Entrepreneurs
- Chamber of Commerce members
- Direct sales companies
- Leaders

Most Requested Presentations:

- Inspired Business Secrets: Marketing Tools to Generate Leads, Increase Revenue, and Build a Thriving Community!

- Act Fast Now: Jumpstart Your Business with the A.C.T.I.O.N. Formula for Success

- Learn How to Catapult Your Business with Heart-Based Communities

- Rock Bottom Is A Beautiful Place

Contact Diane at diane@dianecunningham.com or visit http://nacwe.org/speaking/ to discuss the ideal program for your next event.

Coaching with Diane Cunningham

- Do you need more clients so you can get into higher profits and help your family?

- Are you sick and tired of lying awake at night feeling overwhelmed and like you are never going to "arrive?"

- Are you ready to finally use your God-given gifts and strengths to make more money and start supporting the causes you are passionate about?

- Do you need accountability, guidance, and tough love to stop HIDING OUT and really build a business empire?

In addition to the membership options at the National Association of Christian Women Entrepreneurs, Diane coaches a select number of clients each year, privately and in small mastermind groups.

She provides coaching in person, through Skype, by phone, and at retreat locations. She offers VIP days that get you unstuck, focused, and into action.

If you do not have someone inspiring, uplifting, supporting, and holding a bigger vision for you than you hold for yourself, you will benefit greatly from the one-on-one coaching with Diane.

This is the program to get intense feedback, personalized research, step-by-step training, and accountability. We will work together generating ideas, fixing broken places, thinking of taglines, researching your competition, and helping you to "move the needle."

With her background as a counselor and now as a "business therapist," she helps you work through challenges, mindset struggles, and unhealthy business habits. We create a strategic solution-focused action plan for success in your marketing and your mindset. And we pray at the beginning and end of every session.

The type of client that she loves to work with is:

- An action taker

- Willing to try new things

- Committed to working through the discomfort of change and growth

- On a mission to build the business that God has given them

- Ready to let go of mistaken beliefs and mindsets

Are you ready to get started and discuss the right program for you?

Go to www.nacwe.org/getstarted and fill out the form or email diane@dianecunningham.com.

Are you looking for a business coach who shares your passion, enthusiasm, and faith? Go to www.nacwe.org/getstarted and fill out the information form. Diane will schedule a Get Acquainted Session so you can discuss your options for private coaching.